Moving Images in the Classroom

A SECONDARY TEACHERS' GUIDE TO USING FILM & TELEVISION

Term-time opening hours:

Mon, Tues

 British Film Institute

 English & Media Centre

 FILM EDUCATION

Acknowledgements

Many people contributed in different ways to *Moving Images in the Classroom* and the editorial team are extremely grateful to them all. In particular we would like to mention the following:

Those attending a *bfi* seminar in December 1999, chaired by Professor Dylan Wiliam of King's College, London: Sally Blackwell (Dartmoor Community College, Devon), Geoff Dean (English Adviser, Buckinghamshire), Tony Knight (QCA), John Hertrich (Ofsted), Paul Higgins (National Literacy Strategy), Martin Hollins (QCA), Roland Howard (Gillott's School, Henley-on-Thames), Barbara Jones (QCA), Chris Maynard (QCA), Jane McCarthy (*bfi*), Sarah Mumford (National Museum of Photography, Film and Television, Bradford), Martin Phillips (English and Media Adviser, Devon), Margaret Talboys (QCA) and Mike Weller (English, Drama and Media Adviser, Sussex).

The subject grid contributors:
Martin Hollins (Science), Chris Durbin (Geography), Ian Williams (Design and Technology), Professor Brian Hill (Modern Foreign Languages), Tony Carroll (Art and Design), Kevin Hayter (Music) and Gill Pooley (Citizenship).

Subject Officers at the Qualifications and Curriculum Authority who commented in detail on the subject grids: Jerome Freeman (History), Barbara Jones (Geography), Tony Knight (Music), Chris Maynard (Modern Foreign Languages), Margaret Talboys (Art), John Keest (Citizenship/PHSE).

Production credits

Further comment and advice were provided by:
Louise Spraggon (*bfi*).

Other contributors:
Andrew Burn, David Parker, Tom Barrance.

The editorial team were:
Cary Bazalgette (*bfi*), Wendy Earle (*bfi*), Jenny Grahame (English and Media Centre), Jill Poppy (Film Education), Mark Reid (*bfi*) and Alastair West (QCA).

While the editorial team has tried to ensure that *Moving Images in the Classroom* will be relevant to teachers across the UK, this first edition relates more closely to the National Curriculum in England than to the curricula in the other three nations. We look forward to continuing dialogue with teachers and other colleagues in Northern Ireland, Scotland and Wales, to explore the ways in which future editions can be made more relevant to their curricula.

Cover image adapted from an Eadweard Muybridge photograph sequence.

First published in 2000 by the
British Film Institute
21 Stephen Street
London W1P 2LN

Copyright © British Film Institute

The British Film Institute offers you opportunities to experience, enjoy and discover more about the world of film and television.

British Library Cataloguing in Publication Data
A catalogue record of this book is available from the British Library.

ISBN 0 85170 831 5

Design: Amanda Hawkes

Cover design: Amanda Hawkes

Printed in Great Britain by Cromwell Press Ltd

Contents

Courtesy: *bfi Stills*

Bringing music history alive: Tiny Davies in *Tiny and Ruby: Hell-divin' Women* (Greta Schiller, 1988) from the video compilation *Black Women in Blues and Jazz* available from bfi Video.

Introduction

Why moving images matter

The moving image is a shared and vital global language. Educators are aware of the power of the moving image, whether delivered through cinemas, broadcast, video or online; but throughout the 20th century attitudes differed towards its place in schools. This guide is intended to help build a secure place for the moving image in 21st century education. Critical understanding of film, video and television is becoming an integral part of literacy, and the spread of digital technologies means that the ability to make and manipulate moving images will become an ever more important skill. Moving images are also important in their own right as a valuable part of our culture. Pupils need access to the history and worldwide range of the moving image's achievements in order to recognise what moving images can do, and to encourage their creative ambitions.

Education professionals know that the lives of young people are informed and animated by the moving image. From early childhood, we live in a world saturated by audio-visual texts. Children spend more time with moving images than they do with school work, and through this they acquire an enormous amount of knowledge and experience which some teachers are learning to access and develop. These teachers enthusiastically argue that the ability to analyse a moving image text sharpens pupils' responses to literature and can increase their reading and writing skills. Film and television versions of literary texts or historical events entice further reading and study. In schools which encourage creative moving image work, teachers in many subject areas, including Mathematics, Geography and Science, have seen its value. Pupils can document and communicate their learning in moving images: assembling and selecting evidence, and using digital technology to present an argument or construct a hypothesis. The moving image can often be more appropriate than written texts or still images as a way of presenting ideas or processes, and for some children it offers new ways of succeeding.

Why now?

Some enthusiastic teachers see moving image material as more than just content to be added to the curriculum. They realise that moving image texts have their own complex and unique language which must be understood properly if these media are to be used in schools to their full potential. However, to teach well the analytical and creative skills relating to moving image texts many will need to develop the appropriate expertise in teaching and curriculum planning. Although this will not happen overnight, there are, fortunately, several recent developments that will help in this task.

The, often daunting, technical and financial difficulties of accessing and using moving images in the classroom are beginning to diminish. Substantial UK investment in hardware, software and networks promises not only to deliver moving images to the classroom but also to provide the means of manipulating and exporting them. The costs of both hardware and software are being driven down as the ICT market expands. In addition, a range of governmental and commercial initiatives are being offered to schools to update their equipment and get access to training.

While the full implications of this investment for teaching and learning remain to be seen, the place of moving images in the curriculum has been clarified by the publication in 1999 of *Making Movies Matter.* This influential report of the Film Education Working Group on the future of moving image education in the UK has been widely discussed. In the same year the Revised National Curriculum for England clarified and increased the prominence of the moving image in the curriculum for 5- to 16- year olds. It is possible that new education policies will be formed in the devolved nations of the UK which will also review the place of the moving image in their curricula. There has never been a better time for schools to develop both critical and creative use of moving image texts.

Which part of the curriculum?

As the communications environment continues to change, there is much debate about the nature and range of the basic skills people will need to participate in the society of the future. There is little doubt that print literacy will remain a key competence, but there is also little doubt that other kinds of competence will grow in importance. The ability to analyse moving images, to talk about how they work, and to imagine their creative potential, drawing upon a wide film and television viewing experience as well as on practical skills, could be termed 'cineliteracy'. Like competence in print, number or ICT, cineliteracy will increasingly underpin the whole curriculum.

▶ In **English**, pupils' moving image-based knowledge of genres, narrative structures and character function can contribute to their self-confidence as readers and writers.

▶ Film and television are important primary sources of evidence on 20th-century **history**, and both fictional and documentary treatments of earlier events need to be considered as influential examples of historiography.

▶ Video is used more widely in **Geography** than in any other subject but pupils need to be able to assess its value as evidence about peoples and places.

▶ Pupils need to explore how **music** can enhance or subvert the meaning of visual images, and combine with them to announce genres or create moods.

▶ The **art** world increasingly recognises time-based artforms including film and video, and opportunities to both see and make different kinds of animation should be available to every pupil.

▶ Moving image media enable access to other cultures and can play a key role in learning **modern foreign languages**.

▶ Pupils can explore many of the processes and systems they must learn about in **Science** more easily through moving images than through print or diagrams, and their general knowledge of science is increasingly derived from film and television.

▶ **Citizenship** explicitly requires pupils to consider how film and television contribute to our ideas about social groups and political ideas.

For basic help, start here!

Moving Images in the Classroom is a guide for teachers, departmental subject heads and curriculum managers in secondary schools who want to develop work with moving images. It offers a set of basic techniques, grounded in the realities of today's classrooms and curricula, which can help any teacher, in any subject area, to use moving images more effectively. These techniques can be used by individual teachers, or they could form the basis of departmental or whole-school policies. Teachers and schools who already teach Media will find much here that is familiar, but the purpose of *Moving Images in the Classroom* is to reach beyond the Media Studies specialist to other subject teachers, to demonstrate the potential value of cineliteracy to enhance pupils' performance and broaden their cultural experience.

This guide also offers ways of moving forward where secondary schools want to make a more substantial commitment to moving image education. It includes a new version of the learning progression model, 'Becoming Cineliterate', originally published in *Making Movies Matter*, which can be used as a framework for assessing the development of pupils' learning over time. This model covers all stages of education. We are already working with primary schools to develop techniques and resources appropriate for younger children, and future editions of *Moving Images in the Classroom* will reflect this.

Moving Images in the Classroom has been written by a team of teachers and advisers convened by the British Film Institute, and produced in association with Film Education and the English and Media Centre. It thus draws upon the expertise of three organisations that have been central to the development of media and moving image teaching in the UK for many years. We are grateful to the Qualifications and Curriculum Authority, and in particular the subject officers, for their support in the development of this publication.

We invite all users of this guide to contribute to continuing dialogue about the role of the moving image within a wider definition of literacy, so that future editions can take account of developments in classroom practice and teachers' reflections upon it.

**Website: www.bfi.org.uk
E-mail: discover@bfi.org.uk**

CHAPTER 1

Basic Teaching Techniques

We all know how frustrating it can be to show a video to pupils and get nothing much back in response apart from 'it was boring' or 'I liked the bit where…'. And what kinds of question can you ask of pupils other than 'look out for…'? Using video more productively is not just a matter of knowing some technical terms – though these can help. It depends upon recognising that the moving image has a complex and dense language of its own that we have all learned to 'read' with such ease while not necessarily being aware of our own skills.

The eight basic techniques described on the following pages are designed to help you unravel the codes and conventions of the moving image, and enable you to use a wider range of film and video texts in the classroom. As you and your pupils unpack the layers of meaning, you will be helping them to develop their general skills as more critical, attentive and knowledgeable readers of the moving image.

The techniques are not age-specific. You could use any of them with any age-group depending on the topic in hand, the moving image text you want to base them on, and how far you want to follow through each activity. But you may feel that Techniques 7 and 8 are inherently more sophisticated and thus more appropriate for Key Stage 4. In each of the nine 'subject grids' which follow on pages 13-33, you will find some of these techniques explained and illustrated in subject-specific terms which should bring them to life for you as a subject teacher.

The first three techniques concentrate on the language of the moving image. They offer you ways of encouraging pupils to see how *everything* in a moving image text is saying something, and contributes in some way to its overall meaning. Technique 1, **Freeze Frame**, concentrates on the visual language of moving images. Technique 2, **Sound and Image**, helps pupils see how important sound is in the interpretation of moving image texts. Technique 3, **Spot the Shots**, draws their attention to the editing process. Any of these techniques can be used from time to time in very short sessions to build up pupils' critical awareness of how moving image texts work, and your confidence in using the technique to develop more critical and thoughtful ways of working with moving images.

The next two techniques, **Top and Tail** and **Attracting Audiences**, deal with the ways in which moving image texts are produced and circulated to audiences. Whatever your subject area, it is important to point out to pupils that any moving image text need not necessarily be taken at face value. They should think about where a film or TV programme comes from and whose interests it may be serving, if they are to use its information critically and constructively. **Top and Tail** in particular is a technique you could use quite quickly and informally whenever you use a video, to establish the habit of checking out a text's sources.

Techniques 6, 7 and 8, **Generic Translations**, **Cross-media Comparisons** and **Simulation**, offer you more substantial classroom activities to explore ways of making changes to moving image texts and relating them to other media. In subject-specific contexts these can thus form the basis of coursework pieces at Key Stage 4, or could be used to set up class projects to explore an issue or topic.

Each technique is set out across three columns. The first column describes the activity itself and the second column provides some simple questions, which should help you to start the ball rolling in setting work or guiding whole-class discussion. Learning objectives are listed in the third column. These are moving-image specific, but if you accept our argument that 'cineliteracy' supports any subject, then you should find these useful insights that will contribute to communication and understanding in your subject area.

We have avoided media jargon as much as possible, but the techniques necessarily introduce some simple and useful technical terms, which are explained in the *Glossary* at the end of this book. To use the techniques you will need, at minimum, a VCR with a good 'pause' facility that enables you to view single frames. A 'frame advance' feature would also be useful. Some of the follow-up activities also require ICT software that can handle moving image material; there is more detail on this in Chapter 4 – *Making moving images with digital media*. Overall advice on how to manage moving image work can be found in Chapter 5 – *Managing teaching and learning about the moving image*.

**Above:
Not part of the curriculum: David Bradley in
Ken Loach's first feature film, *Kes* (1969).**
Courtesy: *bfi* Stills

BASIC TEACHING TECHNIQUE

❶ Freeze Frame

▶ Use the video pause button to help the class discuss each shot of a short moving image text or extract (eg 60 seconds long) by looking at and discussing:
  ▷ What they can see in the 'frozen' image; how the elements of the image are positioned in the frame; how lighting and colour affect what is seen.
  ▷ Distance between camera and subjects; camera angle; movement of the camera during a shot.
  ▷ How many shots there are and how the sequence of shots builds up information and ideas or impressions.

Possible follow-up:
▶ Use a storyboard or moving image software to change the order of the sequence or eliminate some shots.

❷ Sound and Image

▶ Cover the video screen and ask pupils to listen carefully to the sound track of a short moving image sequence and describe exactly what they hear in this sequence.
  ▷ Pupils should identify the type of text they think it is and identify and describe all the sounds they can hear.
  ▷ They should then guess at the content and style of the images in the sequence.
  ▷ Finally show the complete sequence and invite discussion about how sounds and images affect each other.

Possible follow-up
▶ Try out any or all of: different music, different sound effects, a different voice reading the same words, or different words; or eliminate any of these elements. Discuss how this affects the ways the images can be interpreted.

KEY QUESTIONS

▶ Why is the shot composed like this? What difference would it make if it were composed differently?
▶ Why is the camera positioned in this way? What difference would it make if it were somewhere else?

▶ What difference does it make if the order of shots is different or some are missing?

About music:
▶ What kind of music is this? What feelings/images does it suggest to you?

About sound effects:
▶ What exactly can you hear and what might it represent?

About words:
▶ What is said and what can you tell about the speaker(s) from their voice(s)?

About silence:
▶ Why do you think the sequence is silent at this point? What might be going on?

About the final viewing:
▶ What difference does the sound make to the sequence? What difference would it make if some elements were missing?

LEARNING OBJECTIVES

Pupils should learn that:

▶ Every element of a visual image can carry meaning.
▶ Visual images can be 'read' like other texts
▶ The position of elements within the image, the colours used, and the lighting, can all affect interpretation.
▶ Camera distance (eg close-up, long shot etc), camera angle and camera movement all affect meaning.

▶ The number and order of shots affect meaning.

▶ Moving image sound tracks can have four elements: music, sound effects, voice and silence. All of these contribute to meaning.
▶ Sound effects are of two types: 'atmosphere' (ie continuous sound) and 'spot effects' (ie short sounds).
▶ Sound – particularly music – can set the 'mood' of a text and establish its generic identity (eg comedy, thriller).
▶ Sound can often do more to 'pin down' the meaning of a sequence than visual images can.
▶ Sound can affect not only the way viewers interpret the images but also what they actually think they can see.
▶ Off-screen sounds can help to create the impression of three-dimensional space.
▶ Silence can also have a powerful effect on the interpretation of a sequence.

❸ Spot the Shots

▶ After their first viewing of a short moving image sequence, pupils guess at the number of shots used.

▶ On second viewing, they mark each change in shot, scene location and sound (use pause button if necessary).

▶ On third viewing they look carefully at how the shot transitions are created (eg cuts, mixes, fades, wipes etc) and whether the sound transitions happen at the same places.

▶ They should also time each shot.

Possible follow-up:

▶ Create a script or storyboard to support their analysis of the sequence. Variations on the sequence can then be hypothesised: eg eliminating shots or changing the order of the sequence.

▶ If the software is available, pupils could digitise and re-edit the shots to try out different sequencing and timings.

▶ How long is this sequence? How much 'story time' does it represent?

▶ What new information or impression is each new shot giving us?

▶ What information or impression does each change in sound give us?

▶ Why is this kind of shot transition used? What difference would it make if another type of transition were used?

▶ Why are the shots of this length? Does the overall time-scheme of the shots build up a rhythm or a pattern? What is the effect of this?

Pupils should learn that:

▶ The number, sequence and duration of shots in a moving image sequence all contribute to its meaning and are created in the editing process.

▶ Screen time and 'story time' are usually different: the editing process 'manages' the story time for us.

▶ Each new shot should provide new information or impressions: shot changes are not merely 'to keep viewer interest'.

▶ The pace and rhythm of editing and the types of transition used also contribute to meaning.

▶ Sound transitions may not match shot transitions: in drama especially they may anticipate them and this can function to maintain or develop moods such as suspense.

▶ Certain kinds of shot sequence are highly conventional: eg shot/reverse shot in a conversation or interview; or a character looking off-screen is likely to be followed by a shot of what they are looking at.

BASIC TEACHING TECHNIQUE	KEY QUESTIONS	LEARNING OBJECTIVES

Pupils should learn that:

❹ Top and Tail

▶ Show the title sequence of any moving image text and use any of Basic Techniques 1 to 3 to help pupils identify its genre and intended audience, and to predict its content and 'message'.

▶ Show the production credits at the beginning and/or end of a moving image text and discuss the information they provide about the source and ownership of the text, how it was produced, and how it was distributed to audiences.

▶ Is this a cinema film or a TV programme?   … AND
▶ Is it fact or fiction?   HOW
▶ Who is it for?
▶ What is it about?   CAN

▶ Who made it?   YOU
▶ Who owns it?
▶ Why might it have been made?   TELL?
▶ What roles were involved in making it?

▶ Title sequences identify the text and 'sell' it to audiences; they may be very explicit about the text's genre, content, audience and purpose or they may disguise this to provoke curiosity.
▶ Information about who made a text, who financed it, and who owns it, can alert you to the interests it represents – and those it may not represent, or may misrepresent.
▶ Many roles may contribute to the production of a moving image text and can affect its content, style and meaning.
▶ A moving image text is likely to be produced by one company and distributed by another.

❺ Attracting Audiences

▶ In pairs or groups, pupils collect information about how a text has been marketed and circulated to audiences: eg TV listings, educational resource catalogues, video catalogues, shop displays, websites, film posters, advertisements, trailers, TV ratings, cinema box office information, reviews, press releases, news items.
  ▷ Groups or pairs present their findings (eg as live presentations, poster montages etc) to the rest of the class, identifying key issues affecting the success or failure of a text to find its audience and convey its message.

▶ What methods were used to promote this text to audiences?
▶ Why were these methods used and not others?
▶ Who helped promote this text and why?
▶ Did audiences respond as the producers intended? If not, why not?
▶ Was media controversy deliberately fostered? Did it help or harm the text? How?

▶ Most moving image texts compete for audiences in a busy commercial market.
▶ Moving image texts can be promoted in many different media.
▶ Marketing and promotional strategies are central to most of the moving image industries.
▶ Most media producers and distributors are part of larger conglomerates and can call upon a range of different companies to help promote their products.
▶ Audience responses are measured and fed back into future production and promotion strategies.
▶ Most moving image production and distribution is expensive and risky.

❻ Generic Translation

▶ Pupils 'translate' a moving image text – eg documentary, TV news item, TV or film commercial, scene from a feature film – into a print genre such as a newspaper item, a magazine feature, an extract from a novel, a short story or a poem.

▶ Pupils translate a print text into moving image form – first as script or storyboard, and then if possible as video (a brief extract or 'try-out' of one scene).

▶ What can you tell in print that you cannot tell or show in moving images?

▶ What can you tell or show in moving images that you cannot tell in print?

▶ Which medium do you think is best for the story/information/ideas you are conveying?

▶ Is a real 'translation' ever possible from one medium to another?

▶ Meaning can change when information is presented in different forms or transposed to another medium.

▶ Each medium has its own language, conventions and genres.

▶ Moving image is more appropriate for some kinds of content or structure, and print is more appropriate for others.

❼ Cross-media Comparisons

Pupils can use Basic Techniques 1-6 to:

▶ Compare the treatment of an issue in two different media and/or for two different audiences.

▶ Compare a key moment from a fictional print text in two different moving image adaptations.

▶ Compare treatments of the same theme in factual and fictional forms.

▶ What elements stay the same and what changes (and how?) for the different audiences?

▶ How do print and moving image respectively manage 'literary' features such as time, character, setting, motivation etc?

▶ What is gained and what is lost in each form?

▶ Groups, issues, values or ideas will be represented in different ways according to the form, genre and intended audience.

▶ Print texts are open to a range of moving image adaptations.

▶ Both documentary and drama can present a theme effectively; the boundary between fact and fiction can be hard to draw.

❽ Simulation

▶ Pairs or groups of pupils are placed in role as producers of an existing moving image text used in any subject curriculum and asked to produce plans for how they would

  ▷ modify or reconstruct it for a different age-group;

  ▷ 'sell' the text to a different audience;

  ▷ challenge it critically from a particular point of view;

  ▷ produce an alternative text.

The plans should be presented to the teacher or another group acting as Commissioning Editor or Executive Producer.

▶ Why have you chosen this age-group/audience?

▶ What in the existing text will not appeal to or be understood by its new audience?

▶ What aspects of the text can you use to sell it to its new audience?

▶ What methods would be most appropriate to reach that audience?

▶ From what point of view are you arguing against the text or for a different version?

▶ What evidence are you using to back up your argument?

▶ Who is the audience for the new version?

▶ Most moving image texts are produced within editorial and institutional constraints: time, budget, context, purpose etc.

▶ Content and form will vary according to audience and purpose.

▶ Addressing a different audience can add ethical or legal factors which will affect what can and cannot be said or shown.

▶ A critical challenge to an existing text must have good evidence to back it up which can come from both within the text itself and from other sources.

▶ Alternatives are possible.

CHAPTER 2

Moving images across the curriculum

Pupils...should...be taught to use the patterns of language vital to understanding and expression in different subjects. These include the construction of...texts that are often used in a subject (for example, language to express causality, chronology, logic, exploration, hypothesis, comparison, and how to ask questions and develop arguments).

The National Curriculum Handbook for secondary teachers in England, DfEE 1999, p40

To use film or television in any subject simply as illustration or motivation is never enough. It misses out on the 'patterns of language' with which moving images communicate information, ideas and values.

A 1990s science documentary about the discovery of DNA and a contemporary news item on the same topic will both be valuable as sources of understanding about the impact of that discovery, but they will also differ significantly in style and ideology. Those very differences could also be part of what pupils need to learn about the development of genetics. A television travel programme about Central Asia and an action adventure film set in the same area will both illuminate pupils' understanding of life, landscape and climate in that region but in very different ways. Pupils will need to understand and describe those generic differences in order to make the kind of comparisons that will enhance their understanding of the subject.

As a subject teacher you can develop pupils' awareness of the particular and diverse ways in which moving images can show processes, tell stories, present arguments and describe places, as well as the ways in which they can mislead or lie. By doing this you will not only help pupils to interpret film and television more effectively, you will help them to understand the role of the moving image in constructing subject knowledge and, indeed, perceptions of what the subject is. This in turn may inspire pupils to use moving images themselves in presenting their learning to others, whether for assessment or simply in order to consolidate and take ownership of what they have learned. In other words, effective use of moving images can help you teach your subject better.

This section of *Moving Images in the Classroom* provides subject-specific guidance in the form of ideas and techniques for working with moving images in nine different curriculum subjects: English, Science, Design and Technology, History, Geography, Modern Foreign Languages, Art and Design, Music and Citizenship/PHSE.

For each subject we have provided two grids. The first presents a rationale for including moving image related activity in your subject area. Learning objectives that situate moving images within the subject are mapped against types of activity and the kinds of outcome that pupils might be expected to produce. We have stressed non-written outcomes, including multimedia presentations, performance, and video production. Although these still present a challenge to the resources and budgets of some schools, increasing numbers are looking to these options and for some this section may help you make the case within your

school or department for resources and training that will support this kind of work.

The second grid for each subject selects some of the basic techniques described in Chapter 1, but this time sets them within the subject specialism. The exemplar activities and tasks are intended not only to develop subject-specific learning but also to enhance pupils' effective use of moving image media within that subject. Not all the basic techniques are used in each grid, but the grids will, we hope, provide you with starting-points to develop your planning.

We have deliberately not specified age-levels against these activities. Most moving image related activities, as described at the level of generality necessary in these grids, can be undertaken at a wide range of age-levels and can be revisited at different stages. Differentiation is achieved through the type of text selected for the activity, the topic or subject matter to be studied, and teacher expectations of the level of analytical skill, viewing experience and independence of thought that pupils may bring to the task. Generally speaking, each grid progresses from relatively simple analytic tasks using techniques like freeze-frame, to more sophisticated activities which may be more suitable for older pupils.

Above:
History represented as myth in David Lean's stunning but enigmatic *Lawrence of Arabia* (1962).
Courtesy: *bfi* Stills

Working with moving images in **ENGLISH**

LEARNING OBJECTIVES

Pupils should learn:

- That moving image versions of literary texts are different from the originals and that each new version of a text will be different, according to when and in what circumstances it was made.
- To 'read' and analyse the language and conventions of moving image texts.
- That moving image and literary versions of the same text may share some features in common, eg aspects of narrative form.

That moving image texts can operate in ways analogous to print texts in their use of metaphor, symbol, and allegory.

- To script and perform in film versions of plays, thus learning that in drama there are many different ways of conveying action, character, atmosphere and tension.
- That in filmed drama, the structure and organisation of scenes can contribute to dramatic effect as well as dialogue and action.

ACTIVITIES

Pupils should have opportunities to:

- Study more than one moving image version of a literary text, and compare how they differ in interpretation through the use of visual and sound conventions, casting, production values, and how they each are shaped by the era in which they were made.
- Analyse the specific ways in which moving image versions of texts achieve their effects – in combinations of image and sound – and contrast these with the ways in which literary texts 'solve' problems of rendering action, setting, character, and narrative voice.
- Compare the way a common narrative structure is realised in moving image versions and a literary source – looking at narrative and authorial point of view, management of chronology and sequence of events, plot structure.

- Identify and explore the equivalents of metaphor and symbol in specific film, video, or TV texts: the use of objects, lighting and colour to signal meanings. Eg a slanting shadow across a face often signifies a troubled or fragmented personality.

Experiment with different ways of interpreting drama for the screen, eg by using different lighting set-ups, different locations, the 'long take' or edited sequences, the close-up, shot composition and choreography.

OUTCOMES

Pupils could produce:

- Shooting scripts for sequences of literary text, which are then contrasted with other moving image versions of the same literary source.
- A 'package' for a new moving image version of a literary text – which identifies cast, director, a script treatment, and marketing campaign.
- A treatment for a condensed TV version of a literary text in which some events are summarised or left out, and others are fleshed out or foregrounded.

- Writing that demonstrates their understanding of the use of symbol in moving image texts.
- Plans, scripts, designs for moving image texts which explore or use metaphor and symbol.
- Short video versions of key poems which find visual analogues for poetic devices.

- Lighting and camera plans, 'test' shots, performed and filmed sequences for extracts from plays.

- That non-fiction moving image texts, like news bulletins, documentaries, and current affairs programmes are mediated presentations of reality, whose producers may intend, but don't necessarily succeed, to produce 'pictures of reality'.

- Summarise the key points and positions of a non-fiction moving image text.
- Distinguish between fact and opinion, examine structural biases in non-fiction programme making, identify elements of moving image language that are used to persuade, argue, explain.

- A TV news bulletin, edited interview, or documentary sequence about an issue covered elsewhere in the curriculum, or arising out of study of a literary text.
- An observational documentary or 'essay' on a topic or theme.
- A video autobiography or edited interview with family or friends to express something about 'personal identity'.

- To recognise and explore the many different kinds of pleasure that can be generated by moving image texts.
- That different individuals and audiences may respond to the same text in very different ways.
- That audience appreciation of a moving image text may relate as much to its fulfilment of generic expectations as to its 'originality' of form or style.

- Identify some of the pleasures offered by particular texts to real audiences and readers.
- Undertake audience surveys, interviews or focus groups to explore reactions to a specific film or group of films.
- Examine how texts are often constructed both to satisfy and thwart audience expectations.

- A shot list or edited trailer for film or TV programme, which identifies the key pleasures of the text.
- A viewing diary and interviews with readers/ audiences to identify differential responses to same or similar text – eg within own family.
- A plot/graph/table of how specific text meets or resists a generic pattern.

Courtesy: *bfi Stills*

Contrasting interpretations
of the same play:
Orson Welles in *Macbeth*
(Orson Welles 1948) and
Toshiro Mifune in
Throne of Blood
(Akira Kurosawa 1957)

Courtesy: *bfi Stills*

Using the basic teaching techniques in **ENGLISH**

BASIC TECHNIQUE	POSSIBLE TEACHING ACTIVITIES	LEARNING OBJECTIVES
		Pupils should learn that:
Freeze Frame	Use the pause button to freeze a frame from each shot of a short scene from a film or TV version of a literary text or Shakespeare play. Pupils must identify how the source material has been interpreted – ie the dress, props and setting, the performance – gesture, facial expression – of the actors, and the composition – camera angle and distance – of the shot.	Everything that is seen and heard is chosen deliberately by director, writer, designer in order to signify specific things.
Sound and Image	▶ Play a two minute extract of the soundtrack of the opening to David Lean's version of *Oliver Twist* (1948) while concealing the image on screen. Students infer elements of setting (time and place, indoor/outdoor), action, character, mood just from the sound components. ▶ Review the sequence, this time with both sound and image, while students note new information presented to them.	▶ Sound and image convey narrative information in different ways; moving images present information via combinations of sound and image. ▶ Sound can be categorised into sound effects, dialogue, music, and silence. ▶ Sound can work to reinforce, motivate or counterpoint action.
Spot the Shots	▶ Pupils watch a film trailer or TV advertisement all the way through, and guess the number of shots used. ▶ While watching it again, they mark each change in shot, scene, location, and sound. ▶ On the third viewing they note the type of transition between each shot, and whether sound is used to bridge the transitions.	▶ Editing is the prime meaning making operation in moving image production. ▶ Length of shot and types of shot transition can determine the space and mood of a moving image sequence. ▶ Very short moving image texts reveal a great deal about the economics of editing.
Top and Tail	▶ Show the title sequences for a selection of TV dramas from different genres including, if possible, some non-UK versions. Encourage students to identify the 'generic markers' for each extract, ie the information offered which indicates which genre they are from – key icons, soundtrack, narrative world. Pupils then predict the content and messages and values of the programmes. ▶ Show the end credits from each programme, and ask pupils to identify information about the source and ownership of the programme, and to speculate about how this might influence the values presented in it.	▶ Although some examples of generic texts may share similarities, these texts will differ from country – and culture – to country. ▶ The end credits of a moving image text contain an enormous amount of information about who produces it, and how. ▶ Making moving image texts is a collaborative process.

Attention Seeking	Invite pupils to collect information to compare how a new mainstream film and a new foreign-language film have been marketed and circulated to audiences via adverts, posters, trailers on TV and at the cinema, reviews, press releases, websites. If possible see both films and compare each one to its marketing 'message'.	▶ The marketing of films depends on the amount of money available to do it. ▶ Low-budget marketing may achieve success through ingenuity and innovation, and big-budget marketing can fail. ▶ Marketing affects audience expectations and hence how they respond to the film.
Generic Translation	Provide pupils with a passage from a literary text – describing a scene or an action, or an extract of dialogue, and ask them to convert the passage into a shooting script – ie a list of shots, itemising camera position, lighting, shot composition, soundtrack, length of shot, and transition. They have to find ways of solving problems posed by, for example, the first person narrative voice, or by changes in point of view: how can these be rendered visually?	▶ Moving image texts present narrative information and handle character and setting in quite different ways from print texts. ▶ Moving image texts can be described using the headings camera, sound, lighting, editing, and *mise en scène*. ▶ We can produce these generic translations because we have learned (unconsciously) how moving images work.
Cross-media Comparisons	Choose a group of people who are represented in the media in distinctive ways – eg victims of war or famine. Pupils collect examples from a range of texts in different media, eg publicity material from famine relief organisations, news coverage from press, radio and television, documentary television. They then identify what each medium can and cannot convey, and contrast the kinds of information derived from each source.	▶ Different media convey ideas and information in different ways. ▶ What is communicable in one medium may be impossible to show in another. ▶ The origins, purpose and intended audience of a text can affect what it can say and what its ideological or moral message may be.
Simulation	▶ Pupils create a 'package' for a film version of a modern novel. Choose the cast, the director, and write a '25 words or less' pitch which positions the film amongst other films. ▶ They 'pitch' their idea to a studio either orally (role play) or in a letter.	Institutional processes, eg casting, marketing, audience targeting, and collaborative production, are likely to change the meaning – often quite significantly.

Working with moving images in **SCIENCE**

LEARNING OBJECTIVES

Pupils should learn:

- How different kinds of moving image texts use different means for representing space – eg in drama and fiction films, news and documentaries, educational programmes and animations.
- That moving image texts with a scientific or quasi-scientific focus often rely on cameras working in unusual – micro or macro – scales.

- That moving image texts can employ a range of different techniques for signalling the passage of time in the representation of scientific processes – eg summary montage, time lapse photography, slow motion.

- That to understand contemporary science-related issues they must collect evidence from a range of sources and that opinions may differ about its interpretation and value.

- That the ways in which scientists and scientific issues are represented in popular moving image forms is, and has always been, an important and contentious issue.
- That the connotations of 'scientist' can range from 'authoritativeness' and 'truth' to 'dangerous obsession'.
- That the representation of 'science' and 'scientists' can be an important way for films and television programmes or advertisements to 'guarantee' truth.

ACTIVITIES

Pupils should have opportunities to:

- Analyse the various ways in which moving image texts can be used to represent space and compare with ideas of what the 'authentic' experience might be like.
- Construct their own representations of space, eg computer generated or animated models of the solar system, or imaginative approximations of planetary surfaces or atmospheres using sound.

- Discuss and analyse key texts with a scientific focus which use time lapse photography, eg *Koyaanisqatsi* (Godfrey Reggio 1983), *Microcosmo* (Claude Nuridsany 1996).

- View clips from different sources on a topical issue, eg global warming, genetic modification, identify the evidence presented, discuss any differences and consider why these have occurred.

- Compare the representation of scientists and science in historically diverse texts, eg *Metropolis* (Fritz Lang 1926), *Dr Who* and a recent advertisement for a product such as cleaning liquid or painkillers. Pupils to identify the conventions that signal 'this is true/reliable', and consider which aspects of 'science iconography' (eg labs, bubbling flasks etc) have changed and which have stayed the same.

OUTCOMES

Pupils could produce:

- Computer model or animated representations of space environments.
- Multimedia presentations on different use of sound and image in different textual representations of space.

- Timelines of 'real time' covered during time lapse sequences.
- Re-edited video sequences where scientific processes are stretched or summarised.

- A multimedia presentation or edited video with voice-over which presents a critical review of the available evidence.

- In groups, pupils produce contrasting scripts for a demonstration of, for example, electromagnets, each group having been given a different stylistic brief (mad obsessive, calmly authoritative etc).

Using the basic teaching techniques in **SCIENCE**

BASIC TECHNIQUE	POSSIBLE TEACHING ACTIVITIES	LEARNING OBJECTIVES
		Pupils should learn that:
Freeze Frame	▶ Select a TV advertisement that depends upon 'scientific evidence' for its sales pitch. Use the pause button to go through the ad shot by shot and ask the pupils to make notes on exactly how the argument is presented through visual techniques. ▶ Pupils could devise their own version of the advertisement – either as a storyboard or as a video sequence – that presents the scientific evidence more objectively.	▶ Moving images can use a range of techniques to present information that appears to be complete and credible but is not. ▶ It is difficult to present scientific evidence in 30 seconds and in a way that will appeal to consumers.
Generic Translation	▶ Pupils view a science documentary, eg on the reactivity of metals, and re-present the information as a magazine feature using print and still images. ▶ They should add a separate commentary on the problems they encountered in the task, ie where concepts or processes were harder to demonstrate in a static medium.	▶ Some things are easier to tell or show in moving images than print, and vice versa. ▶ Meaning can change when information is transposed to another medium.
Simulation	▶ In groups, pupils prepare 'pitches' to a broadcaster who has announced their intention of producing a primetime TV series on science-related issues such as the efficient use of energy, the use of drugs including tobacco and alcohol, or the dangers of 'sound pollution'. Each group must research and prepare a proposal for a programme that will be popular and interesting but also scientifically accurate; one group will act as the executive producer to hear the pitches and decide which ones can be accepted for the series.	▶ There are many ways of selecting and presenting evidence. ▶ A presentation to a popular audience will be different from an academic presentation but can still be accurate.

Working with moving images in **DESIGN AND TECHNOLOGY**

LEARNING OBJECTIVES	ACTIVITIES	OUTCOMES
Pupils should learn:	Pupils should have opportunities to:	Pupils could produce:
▶ The properties of different materials and components can be used in various ways when designing and making a product; these properties and uses can be represented or simulated in moving image text. ▶ Moving images can effectively illustrate the possible weaknesses and strengths in the initial design of products. ▶ Moving image texts can be deliberately used to exaggerate the finish and structure of a product in order to promote the visual impact of its performance. This may have value in marketing the product by encouraging audience empathy for the approach of the designer.	▶ Make comparisons between the working characteristics and applications of a range of items using a computer simulation programme which contains moving images of components (eg gear wheels, pneumatic cylinders). ▶ Look at films or videos that show a product in action – working at its peak (eg racing car) or falling apart (eg bridge collapsing due to wind force). Compare this visual evidence with that from written sources when analysing product performance. ▶ Look at a video of designs in action (eg a fashion show) which may contain slow or stop motion images. Assess how and why techniques such as re-editing, digital manipulation and sound effects have been used.	▶ A film, video or ICT animation presentation which demonstrates the function of components in a design. ▶ Two video recordings of the same designed product in action, one which uses moving image techniques to show off the design to advantage, the other using them to emphasise design faults.
Different kinds of moving image text can provide authentic records of industrial production in the past and present and can stimulate ideas of how to plan production and arrange industrial processes in different ways.	Compare and discuss film or video recordings of a batch or mass production of a range of products (eg food, electrical, textiles) including examples from different times and cultures. Pupils should identify differences in style, content and genre (eg what is and is not shown, voice-over commentary, sources and purposes (Government, industry, political propaganda etc)).	A live or multimedia presentation comparing the different ways in which mass production has been represented at different times, analysing how these styles illustrate cultural, social and ideological values.
Moving image sources such as documentary films, sports coverage, surveillance cameras etc can suggest opportunities for the design of control systems which are to be used in areas where pattern of movement of people is an important factor.	Draw on a range of audio-visual information sources which they can combine with their own practical experience as they design and make their product (eg a computer controlled system to prevent theft, control access or detect tampering in a commercial or domestic setting).	A product which uses moving images as part of the design research process or as part of the marketing of a proposed solution to a design problem (eg in a security system). This could be accompanied by a written evaluation of the design context using stills or a storyboard from a film of crowd movement.

Using the basic teaching techniques in **DESIGN AND TECHNOLOGY**

BASIC TECHNIQUE	POSSIBLE TEACHING ACTIVITIES	LEARNING OBJECTIVES
		Pupils should learn that:
Freeze Frame	While watching a clip from a relevant TV programme, eg *Tomorrow's World*, use the pause button to isolate shots that relate to the evaluation of a process or product that pupils are working on. Ask them to consider why the shot has been set up in this way, and what differences another set-up would make.	Moving images need to be 'read': camera distance, angle, lighting and the place of a shot in a sequence, all affect how the clip is interpreted.
Spot the Shots	After viewing a video of a manufacturing or packaging process, eg extrusion of plastic components or filling bottles with liquid, ask pupils to work in pairs for five minutes to compile a checklist of the stages in the process. Then re-view the video to check how many different camera set-ups and shots were used and whether all of every part of the process needed to be shown.	Timing, pace and editing are essential elements in presenting a concise message about the design context or a proposed solution; understanding this can help people become discriminating and informed users of products.
Spot the Schedule	Show pupils examples of promotional or advertising material based on a product similar to that which they are designing. Discuss with them the purpose of the text and the audience it is aimed at. Ask them to list what parts of the material are fact and how audiences may respond to any part which might not be.	▶ Marketing and promotional strategies are a vital part of product development. ▶ Audience or user response must be carefully measured throughout the design process. ▶ Promoters and advertisers use a variety of moving image forms and approaches to promote products.
Simulation	In groups, pupils discuss the viewpoint, messages and values in a TV advertisement, then plan an alternative text for the same product that addresses moral, cultural and environmental considerations in a different way. One group plays the role of producers who decide which revised approach will be acceptable, and why.	▶ Moving image texts are produced as part of the marketing process of a product for specific audiences. ▶ They are generally constructed within expected conventions but they could be different

Working with moving images in **HISTORY**

LEARNING OBJECTIVES	ACTIVITIES	OUTCOMES
Pupils should learn:	Pupils should have opportunities to:	Pupils could produce:
▶ Historical periods, events and individuals can be represented in different kinds of moving image text: documentary, drama, propaganda, advertisements, home movies, educational programmes. ▶ Different kinds of moving image text can have different values and limitations as sources of historical evidence.	▶ Look for and use internal evidence (eg music, settings, style, characters etc) and/or external evidence (eg title, source) to identify the genre of any text. ▶ Make comparisons between different kinds of text, and refer to generic characteristics, to argue for and against their value as historical evidence.	A live and/or ICT-based multimedia presentation on the Suffragettes, drawing upon a generically wide range of moving image sources from different periods of the 20th century, to explore and explain the kinds of evidence which can be derived from each.
▶ Moving image texts from 1896 onwards are available as contemporary records of events, places and people. ▶ Contemporary fictional material can also have a value as historical evidence. ▶ Moving image texts can be used to re-present the past, either as documentary reconstruction or as fictional drama. ▶ Some documentaries may mix contemporary and modern material, including the addition of modern music or sound effects to silent film (ie pre-1929).	▶ Look for and use evidence from a moving image text, and compare it with other sources, to determine whether or not it is a contemporary record (eg colour vs black and white, objects in setting, costume, quality and style of filming). ▶ Look for visual evidence within the frame for evidence about life in the period; consider dialogue and narrative for evidence about contemporary manners, attitudes etc. ▶ Watch for changes of style that mark boundaries between different sources; or for techniques that mask these, eg fades or colour changes.	Class simulation exercise in which different groups each 'pitch' to a 'producer' for a commission to make a TV documentary about the Western Front in the First World War. Each group to propose different ways of representing life at the Front (eg with or without contemporary film; adding sound and music, or not; using dramatic reconstruction, or not etc). The 'producer' group decides who gets the commission and provides a rationale for their decision.
▶ Some texts are meant to be accurate and authentic representations, and some are not. ▶ Some texts may deliberately mislead the audience about their accuracy or authenticity. ▶ Entertainment values may outweigh historical accuracy in some texts. ▶ It may be possible to argue that a technically inaccurate fictional representation may have a value for audiences by evoking empathy for an individual or a group.	▶ Look for 'modality markers' (ie how true/accurate a text is meant to be), such as genre, title, music, casting, address to camera (or not), voice-over. ▶ Assess whether techniques such as re-editing, addition or deletion of sound effects, digital manipulation etc may have been used. ▶ Make references to specific elements of a text and use analytical and argument skills to make the case for or against the balance between accuracy and empathy.	Following a viewing and analysis of a short uncontextualised extract from a film about the Russian Revolution, for example Eisenstein's *October* (1928), pupils produce a detailed written analysis, with sketches or storyboard 'quotations', to present a case about its reliability as evidence.

Using the basic teaching techniques in **HISTORY**

BASIC TECHNIQUE	POSSIBLE TEACHING ACTIVITIES	LEARNING OBJECTIVES
		Pupils should learn that:
Spot the Shots	▶ While watching a clip from a TV news bulletin, the class marks each change in shot, scene, location and sound. List all the different elements of the clip, discuss the source of each element and think about why it is there. What difference would it make to the overall meaning if certain elements were removed?	▶ Moving image texts are constructed from many different sources. ▶ Every element of a moving image text carries meaning and therefore has potential value as evidence. ▶ News bulletins as a genre have particular characteristics which affect their value as historical source material.
Freeze Frame	▶ Use the pause button to isolate specific shots in a documentary about Hitler (for example as part of a world study after 1900). Ask pupils to describe exactly what they see, noting camera angle, distance of camera from subject, lighting, and exactly what is included in the frame. Emphasise that each is the result of deliberate choices and discuss the reasons for these choices (eg low angle to emphasise dominance, close-ups to show character, vast crowds to show power etc).	▶ Every element of a moving image text carries meaning and producers can manipulate these elements to produce desired effects. ▶ Certain techniques are associated with certain meanings, and this can be recognised in considering the likely contemporary impact of moving image texts.
Sound and Image	▶ As part of a study of religion and the monarchy in Britain 1500-1750, view the film *Elizabeth* (Shekhar Kapur 1998). Pupils then listen to the sound track of the final sequences (from 'I have rid England of her enemies...') and consider the impact of the music (why Mozart's *Requiem*?) and sound effects. Then re-view the sequence, paying particular attention to camera movement and angle, to arrive at an overall judgement about how the film treats Elizabeth's 'virgin queen' image.	▶ Moving image texts use a dynamic relationship between image and sound to create meaning, and this can inflect interpretation in different ways. ▶ Different kinds of text represent historical characters in different ways and have different value as sources.
Generic Translation	▶ Use contemporary print records (eg pamphlets, press) about a particular event (eg the Peterloo Massacre, August 1819) as a basis for scripting, and if possible shooting and editing, a modern TV current affairs item about the event. Pupils should take a particular interpretative position and select 'interviewees' on this basis, considering carefully whose voices could and could not be heard at the time.	▶ All representations of events select and transform material to suit their medium, their audience and their ideological message. ▶ At any period, attempts will be made to control and censor public representations of controversial events.

Working with moving images in **GEOGRAPHY**

LEARNING OBJECTIVES

Pupils should learn:

► Places and issues can be represented in different kinds of moving image texts, such as news, documentary, polemic documentary, drama, feature films, educational programmes.
► Different kinds of moving image text can have different values and limitations as sources of evidence for issues or representation of places.

► Moving image texts vary in their interpretation of places.
► Interpretations may alter perceptions of the viewers.
► Different genres of moving image texts influence the way we feel about people in those places.

► Understanding of audience and purpose is vital in assessing a text's value as evidence.
► They need to be able to identify where opinion is based on evidence and where it is not.

ACTIVITIES

Pupils should have opportunities to:

View two or three short clips from generically contrasting sources such as the BBC *2000* or Channel 4's *Geographical Eye* series, holiday programmes, feature films, news or documentary. Examine how the 'image' of the country is represented by each clip by looking at whether the overall portrayal is positive, negative or balanced.

Undertake a class simulation exercise where pupils are given different producer/director roles and sets of evidence to make a film about a country such as Brazil; eg one group is commissioned by a charity for homeless people wanting to raise money; others make a holiday programme, a natural history channel programme, a human rights organisation, an environmental charity and an urban development corporation. The outcomes are shared and there is a follow-up discussion about how perceptions of pupils have changed as a result of the simulation.

Study an issue such as shopping malls in the UK or tourists in national parks using the BBC series *Investigating Britain*. Pupils first evaluate the effectiveness of the film overall on themselves. On the second run pupils use freeze frame and spot the shots techniques to look for examples of persuasion and of substantiated and unsubstantiated opinion. They write a discussion genre piece for a magazine.

OUTCOMES

Pupils could produce:

A live or ICT multimedia presentation on a country, such as Japan, USA, France, Italy, Kenya or Brazil, showing how the country is represented in different genres of TV programmes.

► A storyboard for a film about Brazil which would illustrate the place from the perspective of the charity with a clear audience and purpose in mind.
► A written reflection of the impact of this exercise on their own perceptions of Brazil and the influence of moving image media on perceptions.

A written analysis of evidence establishing and setting the context for the issue. The written work should clearly and separately represent both sides of the argument and draw conclusions based on evidence.

Using the basic teaching techniques in **GEOGRAPHY**

BASIC TECHNIQUE	POSSIBLE TEACHING ACTIVITIES	LEARNING OBJECTIVES
		Pupils should learn that:
Freeze Frame	While watching a film clip which has strong landscape scenery (eg *Thelma and Louise* to illustrate the landscapes of south west USA) the pupils write down adjectives which will support written description, classifying them into colours, shapes, patterns and textures. They could go on to create a sketch of the freeze frame and a 'wordscape' where words are shaped into the landscape sketch.	▶ Film-makers choose camera position, framing, angle and movement to create a particular impression of landscape, weather and human activity. ▶ Films can be shot in different ways to portray a place. Compare wide sweeping panoramas and big skies with close intimate details such as sweat drenched shirts, or close tangled vegetation.
Sound and Image	▶ While watching a film sequence, without sound, set in a specific location, pupils hypothesise the sounds (and smells) suggested by the visuals. ▶ With another piece of video and three or four pieces of music or sound effects, pupils work in pairs to evaluate the effects of music on the image of the place. They would select and justify the piece of music chosen.	▶ Sound is as influential as pictures in creating an image of place. ▶ The image of the place conveyed in a film is influenced by the nature of the sound tracks. ▶ The atmosphere of the place is conveyed by the choice of music.
Top and Tail	Pupils are given a printout of some of the credits from a diverse range of films about the rainforest or another issue of human impact on the environment (eg natural history documentary, adventure fiction, charity appeal etc). They are shown the tops of the programmes including the first few minutes of the film and they have to match them with the credits, justifying their choices.	▶ The values and attitudes of film-makers, sponsors and production companies can differ and these differences can often be evident in their programmes or films. ▶ Moving image texts targeted at different audiences can have different perspectives on their subject.
Cross-media Comparisons	Pupils evaluate the portrayal of an earthquake or volcanic eruption, comparing a fictional film interpretation such as *Dante's Peak* (Roger Donaldson 1997) with a BBC Horizon documentary and/or the ITV *Savage Earth* on the Mount St Helen's eruption.	Fact and fiction provide different kinds of evidence about natural phenomena: fiction may provide emotional involvement but be unreliable as evidence; documentary may fail to communicate the immediacy of the experience.
Simulation	Pupils are given newspaper and web based sources on a local or national issue, such as eyesores, traffic congestion, pollution or factory closure. Each is given a different role, some representing interest groups and some more 'balanced' reporters. They consider how best to construct the film to convey their argument to that audience. This can be done as a storyboard (eg using a Powerpoint presentation) or it can be filmed and edited.	▶ Evidence used in film is always limited and may be partial. ▶ Different interpretations depend on audience and purpose, and on producers' attitudes and values. ▶ Combining pictures and commentary is a skilled process.

Working with moving images in **MODERN FOREIGN LANGUAGES**

LEARNING OBJECTIVES	ACTIVITIES	OUTCOMES
Pupils should learn:	Pupils should have opportunities to:	Pupils could produce:
▶ That some genres are common to UK culture and that of the country whose language they are studying, and some are not. ▶ That cultural conventions and audience expectations can be different in other countries. ▶ That TV scheduling and film classification may operate differently in another country.	▶ Make comparisons between the different genres they encounter within the target language environment and those they already know in the UK. ▶ See short clips from a range of films and television programmes from the country whose language they are studying. ▶ See examples of that country's film and TV listing guides.	A review guide of films they have seen from the angle of a language learner or a viewing guide with their ideal week's TV programmes from the target country.
About the authentic background to the languages they are studying.	See subtitled cinema screenings of appropriate short or feature films from the country whose language they are studying, eg *La Fracture du Myocarde* (Jacques Fansten 1990), *Les Vacances de M Hulot* (Jacques Tati, 1952), *Le Ballon d'Or* (Cheik Doukoré 1993) *Die Unendliche Geschichte* (Wolfgang Petersen 1984), *Lola Rennt* (Tom Tykwer 1998).	Promotional material or a poster about the film, in the target language.
▶ About contemporary events in the country whose language they are studying. ▶ That films and TV programmes about the target culture from the UK and elsewhere may present misleading information.	▶ See English-language news, documentary and sport programmes to understand the issues which are concerning the local people. ▶ Compare the treatment of international issues with material produced in the UK, such as the discussion about the Euro.	▶ Their own news or documentary video or multimedia presentation about life in the target country. ▶ Listings of 'How do you know you are in …?' based on visual images only.
That visual and paralinguistic factors are an important part of accurate understanding.	Use clues from performance, generic markers, visual style, music and sound effects to help interpret verbal language in simple short moving image texts in the language they are studying.	Use video or ICT to provide a re-voiced commentary to a news item or advert in the target language.

Using the basic teaching techniques in **MODERN FOREIGN LANGUAGES**

BASIC TECHNIQUE	POSSIBLE TEACHING ACTIVITIES	LEARNING OBJECTIVES
Freeze Frame	▶ Use the pause button to focus pupils' attention on each shot of a clip, advertisement or short film: pupils use visual clues from each 'freeze frame' to establish genre, distinguish characters' roles and recount – or perhaps predict – narrative development, using the correct tense. ▶ Pupils can be provided with a list of phrases, some of which appear in the clip and some do not. Pupils play word bingo and tick those they hear. ▶ Use the colour control to convert 'frozen' frames from colour to black and white, and ask pupils to recall and name the colours of selected objects within the frame.	▶ Develop pupils' listening skills and the ability to relate their existing moving image knowledge to the interpretation of the whole text. ▶ Develop pupils' skills in close analysis of a moving image text and the ability to compare texts across cultures. ▶ Develop pupils' awareness of how language and visual images combine to produce meaning in a moving image text. ▶ Develop pupils' use of different verb tenses by enhancing awareness of past, present and future in a text.
Spot the Shots	Pupils watch a short clip twice through and are then given a shot list describing settings, actions and dialogue, some of which appear in the clip and some of which do not. They must identify the ones that appear in the clip and number them in order.	Development of close observation skills and ability to follow structure of clip using visual and aural as well as language clues.
Sound and Image	▶ Show the clip with sound only. Pupils guess the visual content: how many people, what they look like, where the action is taking place etc. ▶ Show a clip with vision only. Working as a class or in small groups, using a prepared framework, pupils reconstruct the dialogue or commentary, orally or in writing.	Pupils integrate their moving image knowledge with their language skills, using contextual sound to help them place and understand the language; or using visual and stylistic clues to reconstruct dialogue.
Top [and Tail]	Show the title sequence and opening credits of a film or television programme in the target language. Pupils have to identify its genre and intended audience, and predict its content or 'message', using moving image analysis skills as well as listening skills. This can be presented as a multiple choice activity if pupils are unfamiliar with the necessary terminology: pupils can be asked to justify their choices.	▶ Develops close listening skills linked to careful analysis of moving image conventions and techniques. ▶ Acquisition of specialist vocabulary in the target language relating to moving images.
Attracting Audiences	Pupils study promotional material for the release of a film they know in the country of the target language: posters, press listings, reviews, trailers. They identify differences and similarities between this material and the film's UK release, and explore the reasons for these.	▶ Broader understanding of the culture of the country whose language they are studying and an awareness of differences in audience expectations. ▶ Further acquisition of specialist vocabulary.

Working with moving images in **ART AND DESIGN**

LEARNING OBJECTIVES

Pupils should learn:

- ▶ Artists respond to the meanings of others' work.
- ▶ Artists sometimes use past work to inspire them to make new products, such as title sequences for arts programmes or advertisements for TV/cinema release.
- ▶ Rhythm, pattern, light and repetition, and the development of themes are important in the structure of moving image materials.

- ▶ Films are sources for research into the lives and works of artists. Some contain documentary evidence; others use actors. In either case a story of the artist is reconstructed.

- ▶ Some moving image texts are made for non-commercial reasons and may be 'experimental'.
- ▶ Audiences discover abstract moving image texts through word of mouth, galleries and museum visits, TV, or from the Internet (as also happens with some forms of music).

ACTIVITIES

Pupils should have opportunities to:

- ▶ Have fun with paintings, prints and sculptures by making them move, using optical toys or ICT animation software.
- ▶ Look at examples of artists' work in moving image media, such as movies by Andy Warhol or the Salvador Dali sequence in Hitchcock's *Spellbound* (1945).
- ▶ Make contemporary interpretations of traditional subject matter, for example a still life, created as a large sculpture, photographed, scanned in and altered.

Investigate the meanings of artists' work by researching influences and by locating historical determinants. Technological aspects such as changing paint technology or the possible connections between painters and film-makers may provide pupils with a focus for their study.

- ▶ See abstract films such as *Colour Box or Trade Tattoo* by Len Lye (GPO Animation).
- ▶ Analyse moving image sequences in terms of technical decisions made and their effects on audiences. Consider why they were made and who they were made for (audience).

OUTCOMES

Pupils could produce:

- ▶ A short animation that brings objects, shapes or people in a work of art to life. Ideas could be developed and later used to design a title sequence for an Arts review programme.
- ▶ A digital still life using different point of view shots and unusual camera positions.

Hypertext links in a multimedia presentation to show a range of influences on and different interpretations of an artist's work.

An abstract film by piecing short lengths of patterns or shapes into a sequence: 8mm or 16mm celluloid film could be edited together by members of a class and later projected onto a screen.

Using the basic teaching techniques in **ART AND DESIGN**

BASIC TECHNIQUE	POSSIBLE TEACHING ACTIVITIES	LEARNING OBJECTIVES
		Pupils should learn that:
Freeze Frame and Spot the Shots	Show an abstract film, eg *Case of Flame* by Kayla Parker, *February 15th* by Tim Webb (Arts Council), and use the pause button to allow pupils time to see the kind of patterns used and the length of each shot.	▶ Experimental film-makers use techniques such as freeze frame, discoloration and jump cutting. ▶ Some moving image productions are not sequenced in a linear narrative.
Sound and Image	Show an animated short film, eg *The Sandman* (1991, Vektor Television)*, or *Growing* by Alison Hempstock (1993, Channel 4). Compare how musical sounds and sound effects (eg creaking stairs) create atmosphere and communicate the story.	Musical and non-musical sounds can both add depth to a moving image text.
Cross-media Comparisons	Research the representation of gender or class in a selection of paintings, prints or sculptures (eg late 18th century). Produce a multimedia presentation portraying two or more preferred interpretative positions.	▶ Representations of gender and class are particular to time and place. ▶ New media technology can portray different points of view about the same artefact or image.
Generic Translation	▶ Look at ad campaigns that have used works of art, eg Magritte paintings used in Walls ice cream ads. ▶ Discuss other ways that art images are used for different purposes, eg in MTV channel idents and the opening credits on *The South Bank Show*. ▶ Compare the intended or original meanings in their historical context. Consider the relationship between artist and patron, the intended audience, and technology used – eg compare *The Great Escape* (John Sturges 1962) and *Chicken Run* (Nick Parks and Peter Lord 2000).	▶ Underground film-making techniques can be seen in highly commercial forms such as music videos and adverts. ▶ The meanings of a work of art can be added to, changed or re-made depending on relations between producer and maker. ▶ Audiences can enjoy visual jokes, parody or irony through making connections between past works and contemporary treatments of them.

Working with moving images in **MUSIC**

LEARNING OBJECTIVES

Pupils should:

Learn how to co-ordinate timing, pace and editing and how a soundtrack can direct a moving image.

▶ Learn how generic forms of music can directly affect and enhance audience response to a character or scene.
▶ Recognise that music can be the unseen psychological influence manipulating the audience reaction.

▶ Learn how ambient sound can be used to create a sense of three-dimensional space and of period.
▶ Learn how to record a location and atmosphere in stereo, and how to balance and mix a sound track.

Learn how to 'sound design', creating and using a range of sounds that interact with and enhance moving images; realise that what we hear in a moving image is not necessarily the same as what we see.

ACTIVITIES

Pupils should have opportunities to:

Make a camera script for guiding three camera operators through a favourite piece of music, taking into account low, medium and high angled shots. Each camera operator must have time to get into position before they go 'live'; solos must be close-up; individual musical 'flurries' should be shown. Edits should be made on the first beat of the bar if appropriate.

Listen to and analyse conventional generic uses of music in moving image drama, eg shock, suspense, comedy, action, romance, and the use of these in incidental music or recurring themes. Pupils work in pairs to list the musical styles as they occur. They should comment on each style's characteristics, making reference to pitch, duration, dynamics, tempo, timbre, texture and structure, and discuss how the music enhances the drama.

List and annotate the sounds in a short extract from naturalistic film or TV drama, distinguishing between those sounds generated by actions or objects in the frame, and those appearing to originate outside the frame. Discuss the ways in which the soundtrack has added unseen detail, establishes setting indicates time of day and weather and places a scene in a specific area or region. Pupils should listen for electronic enhancement (eg reverberation or echo) and consider why this has been used.

Subvert or extend the meaning of a moving image clip by re-designing the sound track with sound effects that are not motivated by anything within the 'world' of the film (whether on-screen or off). The new track should retain precise timing and pace but also add a new dimension to the atmosphere (eg suspense, sorrow, menace).

OUTCOMES

Pupils could produce:

▶ A finished camera script for live recording of a music performance including floor plan to show camera position and movement.
▶ A video version of a school group playing a piece of music, using ICT software to edit the video to the music.

A group or individual composition of specific length that portrays or enhances the atmosphere of a scene: suspense, romance, comedy, performed in synchronisation with a film clip. Some groups or individuals could change the style to subvert the meaning of the clip. In either case the results should be discussed and analysed by the group.

▶ A finished recording of an atmospheric sound track which uses the effects of stereo (eg bowling alley, football match, approaching train), performed to the rest of the group for identification.
▶ Performance of a correctly mixed and balanced recording which recreates an historical period, based on research on changes in everyday sounds both inside and outside the home.

Design and record a sound track for a clip from a silent film melodrama, using non-realistic sounds and musical tones to heighten the emotional effect and dramatic tension.

Using the basic teaching techniques in **MUSIC**

BASIC TECHNIQUE	POSSIBLE TEACHING ACTIVITIES	LEARNING OBJECTIVES
		Pupils should learn that:
Spot the Shots	Analyse a video of a group performing with instruments, using the pause button to help identify the number of cameras used and the number of shots. They then consider the relationship between the shot changes, the beat of the music, the riffs within the music and the solos within the riffs, and discuss why it has been done this way.	Shot changes and camera position can enhance the meaning of a music video and affect how it is interpreted by audiences.
Generic Translation	Add generically different music to subvert the meaning of an advertisement, title sequence or short extract. For example follow one episode of a popular Australian soap opera, noting the incidental music played at the end of scenes following the end of dialogue, while actors hold poses before a cut or fade. This music may only be three chords or two held notes. Discuss the effect in relation to dialogue and pose: mystery, romance, danger etc. Pupils compose their own end-of-scene music to subvert the meaning or mood (eg romance to danger, mystery to comedy).	Generic music can help to 'anchor' the meaning of a moving image text; changing the genre of the music may or may not shift the genre of the whole piece.
Top and Tail	Pupils study the front and end credits of a feature film and identify the roles and tasks involved in the creation and provision of music for a full-length film, and compare the film's use of music to the soundtrack CD. They find out how much of each track is actually played in the film and explore the relationship between the film's financiers, the distributors, and the music rights-holders.	▶ There are stages in creation of music for feature films and the process is complex. ▶ Films can be successfully promoted with the release of a title track into the popular charts. ▶ Soundtrack CDs may contain just a compilation of pop records and not the music specifically written for the film.

Working with moving images in **CITIZENSHIP/PSHE**

LEARNING OBJECTIVES	ACTIVITIES	OUTCOMES
Pupils should:	Pupils should have opportunities to:	Pupils could produce:
Understand that images of women and men are constructed by the media and convey certain messages about gender and body image.	Develop the tools to deconstruct a moving image text (eg an advert or an extract from a feature film) in relation to gender or body image. Students should look for camera angles, voice-over, expressions, stance, age, appearance, juxtaposition of images and sequences.	A live or multimedia presentation using examples from film, TV drama, adverts and documentary to argue the case for or against the role of the media in encouraging eating disorders.
Learn that common stereotypes and forms of prejudice can be reinforced by some moving image texts or challenged by others.	Compile representations of a specific social or ethnic group and investigate audience responses to them, using techniques such as questionnaires, interviews, focus groups.	A video montage drawing on a range of moving image texts representing aspects of disability, with a commentary evaluating the force of both positive and negative images.
Learn how to identify bias and emotive and persuasive techniques in moving image news and documentary, and understand how these may influence public opinion.	Collect and compare a range of news and documentary texts to analyse current social values in relation to a specific issue, eg asylum seekers, crime, drugs, poverty, hunting etc. Analyse the presentation and compare styles between different channels, and identify the use of bias through exaggeration, emotive language, voice-over and images used.	A video news item in the style of a chosen news programme on an issue of their choice. Pupils use techniques learnt to slant their item so that it reflects a specific point of view.
Learn that dominant conventions of representation can change over time, and about how and why this can happen.	Look at past coverage of a specific group, institution, event or issue (eg the family) and compare it with present-day coverage, identifying similarities and differences and accounting for these.	A letter to a commissioning editor or production company to criticise coverage of an event or issue and suggest ways in which it could have been done differently.
Discover the potential of moving image media to represent themselves and/or their group in a positive and effective way.	Look at home videos and other representations of themselves and people like themselves, discussing the positive and negative aspects of the ways they have been represented.	A 'video diary' style presentation of their daily life or a special event.
Know about some of the ways in which government and other agencies use the media to try to influence the public.	Evaluate the use and effectiveness of moving image texts in a pro-social campaign such as safer driving, healthier lifestyles etc.	Re-edited version of an advertisement, public health announcement or party political broadcast, using ICT to cut or re-order the sequence, and/or add different voice-over or music.

Using the basic teaching techniques in **CITIZENSHIP/PSHE**

BASIC TECHNIQUE	POSSIBLE TEACHING ACTIVITIES	LEARNING OBJECTIVES
		Pupils should learn that:
Sound and Image	Show a television charity appeal with the screen covered to focus attention on the sound. The class predicts the images used, then view the whole advert and discuss their predictions. Comment on what is added by the images, how views may be altered by the addition of images, how emotions may be affected by the images.	▶ Moving image texts use a dynamic relationship between sound and image to create meaning. ▶ Producers manipulate images and use a range of techniques to provoke emotion, to persuade and to influence opinion.
Top and Tail	Pupils make notes on the opening and/or end credits for two contrasting documentaries covering a similar issue. They use promotional material such as video covers, TV listings, catalogue entries, and Internet sources, to find out as much as possible about the sources of each documentary, who owns it, and how it has been promoted and distributed to audiences. They then consider the extent to which this information may account for the differences between the two.	Information about who made a text, who financed it, and who owns it, can alert us to the interests it represents, and those it may not represent, or may misrepresent.
Simulation	In groups, pupils take on the following roles: film classification examiners, concerned parents, teachers, children, anti-censorship campaigners. Groups watch a chosen film and draw up a list of arguments (in role) as to how the film should be classified. They must support points made with examples from the film and other supportive evidence. A debate is held to decide on the classification, groups argue their case and a chair makes the final decision. (Groups may be given other supportive materials such as audience effects research and newspaper stories about copycat crime.)	▶ A critical challenge to a text must have good evidence to back it up. This can come from inside the text itself or outside. ▶ Ethical and legal factors will affect what can and cannot be shown in a film aimed at children.
Freeze Frame	Use the pause button to enable pupils to discuss each shot of a chosen advert that uses a woman to sell a product. Draw attention to deliberate compositional choices including lighting, colour, camera angles and distance, pose, the woman's appearance and how she is positioned within the frame and in relation to other objects and people. The choices should be accounted for and alternatives considered. This can then be compared with an advert that uses a man to sell a product or another advert for a similar product.	▶ Every element of a visual image can carry meaning. ▶ Moving images can be 'read' like any other text. ▶ Conventional ideas about women and men can be reinforced by moving image texts.

CHAPTER 3

Using moving images in the classroom
Arguments for and experiences of teaching with moving images

Creativity with moving images
Andrew Burn
Parkside Community College, Cambridge

Creative work with moving images can take many forms: a group of Bengali teenagers making a film with a professional film-maker about their lives, pleasures, culture and identities; the primary school children animating *Red Riding Hood*, complete with a rich knowledge of this textual tradition and a range of cartoon-like visual styles; 14-year-olds making trailers for *The Matrix*; two boys making a witty documentary about their visit to a press screening of *Gladiator*, with throwaway remarks about Ridley Scott's filmography, and an interview with the cinema manager about distribution. What is really going on when children undertake these kinds of creative work?

Creativity is an aesthetic human activity. It provokes emotional responses, or those emotional responses peculiar to engagement with fictions – what the American philosopher of film, Noel Carroll, calls 'art-emotion'. This isn't enough, though – unlike Carroll, I would always want to see this kind of aesthetic engagement in social terms: kids make film for themselves, collaboratively with others, for known and unknown but predicted audiences, expressing social understandings, and socially-formulated aesthetic tastes and preferences. When they choose a dissolve rather than a wipe as a transition between two clips in their film, this is an aesthetic preference within a set of generic conventions and tastes that are inseparable from their social and historical contexts.

Creativity is linked with identity. In a sense, every film made by a child is not so much an expression of their identity as a creative attempt to transform it in some way. We could call this a kind of enunciation: the child is saying, 'this is how I see the world'. Or it can be a polemic, as in a short documentary on Clause 28 made by some pupils at Parkside recently. It can be an even more direct reworking of the stuff of identity – one's own image, reworked through the infinite plasticity of sound and image in a digital environment. I watched one of my Year 10 pupils, not confident with much of school, editing a basketball sequence for a sports TV programme for our local cable channel. It featured him as the star player; and his work on his own image, using the grammar of black and white, slow motion, voice-over and a hip hop soundtrack, seemed to me nothing less than a piece of intensely pleasurable creative self-transformation.

Creativity, in moving image work, is caught between the individual and the collaborative. It is inevitably social, but it is easy to get caught in a kind of oscillation between an individually authorial kind of creativity, and different kinds of collaboration. The gap between children good at ICT and those less good at it (often linked to possession of home computers) exacerbates this problem. Many young people who are already excited by the moving image use the digital control offered by the new technologies to enhance their skills at a tremendous rate.

We shouldn't allow this ability to become naturalised or mystified, like some digital throwback to post-Romantic notions of artistic genius. Most of the elements involved – ICT competence, visual design, the grammar of the moving image,

a familiarity with the conventions of a range of film and TV genres – are easily identifiable and teachable, at least in principle. There may or may not be an artistic/creative ability beyond these elements; it's not particularly helpful to assume there is. On the other hand, a good deal of the creative work we do is more collaborative – two pupils at a workstation, one with the mouse, one using keyboard commands, both pointing excitedly at the screen, their discourse of editorial decision overlapping and fusing. Or the primary school children sharing images on a common network space, making their animations in pairs, but dependent on the sequence that comes before and after their own.

Following the DCMS/DfEE report, *All Our Futures*, creativity has become a fashionable new buzzword in education circles. Policymakers must recognise that teachers need a great deal of dialogue and reflection on their practice before we are confident about what we mean by it and how it can be fostered. Practical work with moving images is an interesting and rewarding way of doing this. One thing we can do is continue to explore the analogy between language and the moving image: both are 'semiotic practices' – ways of communicating which can be analysed and taught. They are also both creative in the widest sense, the stuff out of which social identities and participation are made.

Cut-out and jointed figures and semi-opaque backgrounds are used with extraordinary fluidity in Lotte Reiniger's *The Adventures of Prince Achmed* (1923-26).
Courtesy: *bfi* Stills

But maybe this language model has the disadvantage of restricting us to pedagogic traditions of the English classroom. Another obvious source of experience in working with moving images is Media Studies, but its space for creativity has always been ambivalent. Since most exam syllabuses in Media are still rooted in the teaching of interpretive frameworks and critiques of the mass media, the idea of creativity in media production is often buried beneath syllabus imperatives to teach about media forms, representations, audiences, institutions. The idea that a creative practice can justify itself, a familiar idea in the pedagogies of Art and Music, is really absent from Media Studies syllabuses and assessment practices.

We need to recover the wider view that recognises the importance of creativity and pleasure in the making of moving image texts. This must mean looking at the creative practices of the other arts subjects: the visual and textual narratives of Drama, on which, of course, most moving image texts encountered by our students are based; the compositional practices of Music; a time-based medium like film; the visual grammar of Art; the more condensed movement sequences of Dance.

Keeping the creative potential of Media and ICT teaching in the frame, alongside the literacy teaching of English, we need to plunder the pedagogies of the other arts until we find patterns of teaching and learning in which the making of moving image texts can offer a set of creative repertoires to our students alongside the kinds of text they can make with paint, body, sound, and digital inscription elsewhere in the curriculum, and elsewhere in life.

Moving images in Music
K. R. Hayter
Robertsbridge Community College, East Sussex

Because of film set noise, most dialogue and sound effects in live action films are re-dubbed in the recording studio after filming. Animation has no production sound so all sounds are created from scratch. The process of adding the sounds of footsteps, body movements and props is called **Foley**. This classroom activity consists of creating and performing – and perhaps recording – a Foley score for a film or animation extract. It is suitable for all ages from 8 to 16 and upwards: there is plenty of scope here to differentiate the work to suit all abilities and ages.

The exercise must be based on a suitable short clip from a live action or animated film. In order to make this account explicit and precise, I am basing it on *The Angel and the Soldier Boy* by Alison De Vere, with music by Clannad (BMG video 790329). This superb 25 minute video demonstrates perfectly how music and sound can be synchronised precisely with the action. The 62-second clip I would select is 13 minutes into the film: a scene beginning with a drunken pirate captain who climbs into his bunk and falls asleep. The Angel and the Soldier then borrow his keys, open the treasure chest and retrieve a stolen coin.

▶ Play the clip without sound, at least twice.

▶ Divide the class into groups of 6-8 pupils. Each group must create Foley sound effects in perfect synchronisation with the visuals. One student in each group could be responsible for dubbing the drunken pirate's voice on to the soundtrack, paying close attention to mouth movement sounds.

▶ Each group creates their own Foley score for the clip. (See example of Foley Score below.) They must list all body movement and prop-handling sounds in order and time them against a stop clock for precision. The stop clock could be started at the first sound that needs to be precisely synchronised, ie when the bottle smashes. Run the clip as many times as is needed to complete the list.

▶ The groups must now find ways and suitable objects to recreate every sound required. This could be continued as a homework task – for example without using broken glass (obvious health and safety reasons) recreate the sound of a smashing bottle. Pupils can make a recording and/or bring in the effects for demonstration.

▶ Groups will now have a number of options depending on the equipment available. While the film clip is repeatedly shown without sound, each group could simply take it in turns to perfect their sounds synchronised with the action. In addition, a simple piece of music could be played on a keyboard, live or sequenced, throughout the performances. Better still, 3-5 microphones above the props table could be used via a mixer/amplifier to boost the volume of the quieter sounds.

▶ Experiments with microphone placement will reveal how a sound can take on a totally different characteristic when recorded close up. For example: hit a cymbal, wait a few seconds then put your ear or microphone close to its edge. It will now sound like a deep bell. Feeding the microphones into a mixer will allow greater control over balance and sound placement in the stereo field. (Left, centre, right or moving.) Correct line of sight between eye, Foley score, hand, object, microphone and TV monitor is essential.

Foley Score (Running Order)

▶ Starting point of clip: drunken *pirate captain chuckling.*

TIME (Secs)	SOUND REQUIRED	SUGGESTIONS FOR SOUND EFFECTS
	Chuckling	One student in each group could cover all vocal noises – chuckling, mumbling, crying, snoring, yawning etc.
	Clink! Clink! (Hook against bottle.)	Tap a bottle with a metal pen.
00	Smash! (Bottle breaks.) START STOP-CLOCK	Drop open cake tin filled with small pieces of metal, eg small glockenspiel notes and coins.
03	*Crying.*	
12	Footsteps.	Knuckles on prop table/desktop.
15	Keys.	Bunch of keys or chain.
20	*Snoring begins.*	
30	Sword drawn.	One glockenspiel note being dragged across another.
35	Cutting (sword through rope) – 5 cuts.	Gently rub together two pieces of paper close to the microphone.
38	Keys and key into lock.	Bunch of keys or chain. Tap something metallic against a retractable metal ruler case or use a door lock.
44	Treasure chest opens. (Magic)	Wind chimes/chime pipes.
52	Coin put down. *Pirate wakens.*	Gently tap edge of microphone once.
56	Coin rolled twice.	Drag drum stick across serrated edge of wooden guiro.
62	Treasure chest closes shut.	Twist cork in bottle (creaking sound). Gently hit prop table with closed fist (thumb uppermost).

▶ Where equipment is available, groups can actually dub their sound on to the clip. Many VCRs will allow you to dub a soundtrack over existing footage, so groups could record the sound effects in sync with the film clip using a suitable stereo mixer directly onto the video tape soundtrack. Alternatively, non-linear editing software like Adobe Premiere (on a PC) or iMovie (on an Apple iMac) can be used to digitise the clip and the Foley score, and to edit them together.

Undertaking this work shows pupils how powerful sound can be as a component of meaning, and extends their skills and ingenuity in creating credible effects from unlikely sources. It will also develop co-ordination between eye, ear and hand (and brain!).

Moving images in Art
Tony Carroll
Boundstone Community College, West Sussex

The two portrayals below are dramatised accounts from two teaching episodes. The first is based on current work in the school where I have been teaching for one year; the second is based on memories and pupils' work from a few years ago in my last school, where media in Art was already established. The names of pupils have been changed to hide their identities.

I showed my Year 9 group a short film called *The Sandman* (*Media in Art* pack, *bfi* 1996). The aim was to search for understandings in the film's language by responding to different elements such as lighting, characters, colours, sounds, camera angles, and moods. After watching the film there was a strange hush and I wasn't sure of the pupils' reactions to it. I left this pregnant pause and went just to the right of the TV to the security of my whiteboard, where I began writing down some of the headings. The pupils' then started citing examples faster than I could write them down. 'There were shadows on the wall' one shouted, 'and on the door handle', said another. One pupil remembered that a shadow appeared on the boy's face as he lay in bed. When he woke it turned out to be his mother, not the evil Sandman as the music led us to believe.

These pupils told me that in this film blue was used around the staircase and in the bedroom because it was cold and scary. I asked them if blue was always used in this way in adverts or films they watched. They said no, because blue sometimes means fresh, bright and clean, as in toothpaste commercials (and I remembered the blue-white of a washing powder ad). So I asked, 'What did red symbolise in *The Sandman*, or orange-brown?' 'Red was for blood' they all called out, 'when the Sandman pulled out the boy's eyes.' 'Did you actually see it?' I asked. 'No', said Hayley, 'it was shot on the walls in shadows.' 'Ah', I said, 'then it needs to go under the "Shadows" heading as well as the "Colours" one. …Where did we see orange-brown?' 'In the living room,' came the reply.

I then wanted to know what they thought these colours were used for, what they symbolised. Jon reminded us about red, and a few shouted about the blue being cold, before Mark advanced the idea that the living room was warm but the bedroom was cold. Then we realised that the little boy felt safer in the warmth of the living room but more vulnerable in the stairway and bedroom. The mood created by the music and sound effects helped. Pupils referred to the ticking clock and the boy banging his toy drum in the living room. As soon as he went up the long twisted staircase the mood changes by use of musical sound, high pitched notes of a piano and chilling violins, and the non-music sounds like the creaking stairs.

Through this activity the pupils initially made an illustrated spider diagram to extend their design skills and show off their knowledge of the language of this film. Later we made connections to German Expressionist prints to look at the influences on the film's design, such as the distorted bed, clock, door and window. This link helped to place *The Sandman* in the tradition of grotesque tales.

I am currently teaching this group to make a video cover for the film. Considerations of the symbolic importance of colours and shadows are being highlighted as part of the design process where an audience is implied. This is my first year in the school, and in time I would like to be able to set up facilities where video and multimedia work could be carried out.

A few years ago at my last school, low budget video equipment was available after a commitment was shown by the school to support the development of media in Art. I remember a Year 8 class using two video cameras in the art room to record different types of shot from a still life group. I noticed how they worked as a team. Hannah who always used to complain about not being able to draw suddenly became the team leader and I pictured her in a drama lesson where her real talents could come to the fore. In my Art lessons where drawing took place other pupils shone, but with group work activities pupils such as Hannah could shine too. The group made quick decisions to shoot the still life from above, below and from different 'square on' positions. They sometimes zoomed in so close that the object could not be easily recognised. In the editing room later we talked about the rhythms that could be created by the speed of cutting from one shot to another. Martin made a sequence of photographic stills using the same kind of principle about camera position and angle to suggest abstract movement. We then watched *Digital Still Life* by Malcolm le Grice (*Media in Art* pack), and the pupils began to see how someone made art, using ideas about time and visual 'music' to organise their images.

Tony Carroll **Media in Art** Book and Video pack, *bfi* 1996

Moving images in Geography

Chris Durbin

County Inspector for Geography, Staffordshire LEA

Why is the moving image so important in Geography?

Teachers believe that moving images:

▶ enable pupils to 'encounter' images of places they wouldn't otherwise see;

▶ increase the sense of place by communicating the sights and sounds;

▶ combine images with graphics to explain change over time and space in a visual way;

▶ enable pupils to observe (and sometimes hear) real people from the places they are studying;

▶ report disasters, natural or human to a wider audience so that pupils can appreciate the human experience;

▶ explain issues often in a polemic way which allows pupils to see a greater number of perspectives.

However, many teachers do make full use of the visual dimension of moving images. In a revealing experiment (Roberts 1987), groups of student teachers were asked to take notes from a video about Brazil. The transcript of the commentary was read back to them after this note taking exercise. The student teachers were asked to cross out any sentences, phrases that were from the commentary. The majority had no notes left. In other words the act of note taking had for the most part become an auditory and not a visual experience; most of the images were not transferred into words. A single viewing and note taking process allows no time to dwell on the images, and words to express the sense of place are much more easily gleaned from the 'expert' commentator.

Learning objectives for the use of video can be made more explicit by deploying a variety of 'watch' and 'do' exercises,

depending on which of the above objectives is central. By 'do', it might be watch and think, write, discuss or even draw. This approach allows the teacher to focus the watching and then give the pupils time to think and respond. The basic techniques offered in Chapter 1 can help you do this.

Why should Geography teachers teach media? Firstly, it is important for both teachers and pupils to know what their 'geographical imagination' is and where it comes from. Secondly, globalisation is a now a fundamental and pervasive cultural process. Thirdly, moving image media exert a great influence on our perceptions of places. Television programmes and films, whether documentary or drama, create a condensed and often exaggerated perception of place. For example David Attenborough, crawling through the canopy of the rainforest, 'bottles' the scene using very good ecological researchers and very skilled camera operators, and then edits hundreds of hours of filming into a 30-50 minute documentary, which almost always excludes encounters with the actual people who live there.

Perceptions matter: they influence individual and collective decisions. People have perceptions of the world they live in which affect the decisions they make. They choose to live, shop or spend a weekend in a certain place because of the way they perceive it. The driving force behind economic migration is the perception that other places are better, but for new economic migrants the reality is often disappointing.

Moving image media help to create the 'geographical imagination'. Perceptions of places have been called the 'geographical imagination' (Massey 1994) and this varies from person to person, social group to social group, culture to culture. In any one person, this geographical imagination depends as much on personal attitudes and values as well as on the reality of the place itself. Culture plays an

important part in determining this imagination, as do the values and attitudes of family and friends. But most people experience a limited range of places even today with modern travel and therefore visual media influence their 'geographical imagination'. Advertisers of holiday destinations portray a place as tourists wish to perceive it.

Globalisation means more dominance of English language media. Globalisation has had its impact on perceptions of places too. Young people are brought up with images of places from all over the world. For people in the UK this means moving image texts which are British interpretations of distant places, whether they are serious like programmes by Michael Palin or David Attenborough or less so like programmes such as *Caribbean Uncovered* or *Eurotrash*. In the late sixties and seventies, *Blue Peter* presenters went on their 'holidays' once a year. Today young people see global reports from *Blue Peter* at least once a week. It also means more media from other English speaking countries and our perceptions of the USA are often in much greater detail because of the sheer volume of media from that country.

Like land- and city-scapes, worldviews are shaped. Learning with moving image media is important to the moral and cultural education of the pupils in schools. When a teacher puts a visual image of a place in front of pupils, their values and attitudes are used to interpret the pictures, sounds and sequences. We have the means as Geography teachers to make pupils aware of this and to develop their own creative and interpretative skills to convey ideas and information about places and people.

NOTES

Roberts, M. 1987 **Using Video Cassettes**, Teaching Geography vol 12 no 3 pp114-117.

Massey, Doreen 1994 **Space, Place and Gender** Polity Press.

CHAPTER 4

Making moving images with digital media

As accessible and relatively cheap software for the manipulation and editing of moving images comes on to the market, some schools have started to use it within the curriculum. In this chapter teachers explore the way ICT software can be used to develop the practical and creative side of moving image education.

Production work in a specialist school
Andrew Burn, Parkside Community College, Cambridge

Parkside Community College in Cambridge is a specialist media college, under the DfEE's specialist schools programme. Part of our aim is to explore the use in education of the moving image, and of how children both read and respond to moving image texts; and also how they might produce these themselves. We have aimed to explore this across the age range as much as possible; and across the secondary curriculum. For the past three years we have been using a non-linear editing package called *Media 100*, and a cheap animation package called *The Complete Animator*.

Media 100

Media 100, which runs on Mac G4s, is a professional digital video editing package. It imports video footage from any source – we use mainly VHS and digital videotape (DV). It will also output to any format – useful for classrooms which are still equipped with VHS players. The package provides the usual kind of video editing screen. There is an edit window, where the edited footage appears in real time, with some realtime effects (dissolves, colour, lighting and

contrast changes). Other effects (wipes, slow or fast motion, titles) have to be rendered, which can take up to a minute. There is also a window showing the clips of digitised footage, identified by the first frame of the sequence. The editing is done on a timeline, with a two-track video line, and up to four audiotracks below it.

**Above:
'Where does this one plug in?' – a question that is never asked in *The Matrix* (Andy and Larry Wachowski 1999).**
Photo: Jason Boland; courtesy: Warner Brothers

***Media 100* screen: Year 11 trailer**

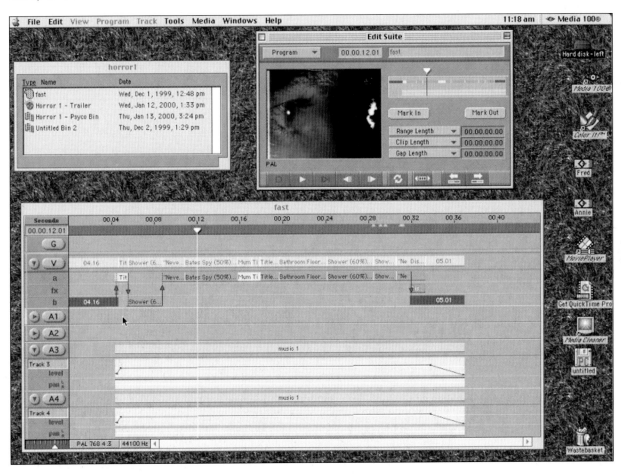

What we use it for

Student projects using *Media 100* have included Media Studies coursework projects (adverts, pop videos, film trailers); documentaries made by pupils (one on coastal erosion on the North Norfolk coast; a number on global and ethical issues); making college anthems (the videos of three rock songs by pupils); making animations combining GCSE music and media work. We have also used it to edit half hour TV programmes we broadcast once a week on local cable TV.

Learning outcomes

We use the package with pupils within a context informed by moving image pedagogies. That is, we have explicitly taught pupils about the forms they are working with, such as the genres, which partly determine how information is communicated, or how narratives are constructed, or the particular effects on audiences invited, by documentary, pop video, and so on.

We have been less clear about how to actually teach the technical procedures of the software. We have tried whole class teaching of the basic structure of the package before they use it; and we have tried small group instruction as they use it. We have been partially successful, not least because of the contribution of highly-skilled technical staff. We need to develop more worksheet based resources, so that pupils can work at their own pace; and more differentiated strategies, partly to address widely differing ICT competences.

Pedagogy

We have aimed to treat the digital editing process as a kind of literacy, though this is not yet very evident in our styles of teaching. We rely too heavily, maybe, on intuitive patterns of learning. These obviously are important, and are one reason why we chose this software – it is intuitively accessible, especially at its most basic level.

Literacy related activity is most obviously to do with processes of redrafting. The technology allows for rapid and easy repositioning of clips on the timeline, trimming and extending clips by grabbing their ends and pulling, and similar editing and positioning of audio clips relative to the video sequences. At their best, pupils deploy wide ranging understandings of how these processes make meaning and affect audiences in moving image texts.

We are aware, however, of the need to make these understandings explicit, to find out who has them and who, perhaps, doesn't share them to the same degree; to problematise the idea of 'intuition', and again, ask who does and who doesn't have an intuitive grasp of these processes. We can then get a clearer sense of what teaching and learning styles will address this breadth of competence.

Achievements so far

The software has been quite easy to teach, especially with children at home with ICT – and we have found this with pupils across the secondary age range. Pupils have been highly motivated by the ability to produce professional quality video, and the speed of the real time editing. This has included, as we originally hypothesised, a number of underachieving boys in the 14-16 age range. Also, we think the software does introduce a new kind of literacy, or at least a new kind of audio-visual communicative practice, which enlarges the menu of forms of expression we can offer our pupils. This can be added to print literacy, kinaesthetic forms of communication, music, and visual communication through the still image in art and photography.

Problems

The original cost of the package was prohibitive to any but specialist schools with additional funding; however, the cost has now come down steeply, and a single workstation with the *Media 100* LE (entry level) software is now about £5000. This, at five times the price of a top end PC, is still a heavy investment for an average sized or small secondary school; but within the reach of a larger school, especially one with a large Media Studies post-16 programme.

Related to the cost, the number of workstations imposes limits on the use of the equipment. One workstation would allow use by small specialist groups – perhaps a GCSE or A level Media Studies group. Production groups of about four would need to use it in rotation. We have gradually acquired five workstations, which allows for more extensive use in different subject areas and with four Media Studies groups in the 14-16 phase.

The hard disk storage space can be a limitation; this is also a cost issue. Within six months, we needed to double the amount of storage space available. We now aim for 18 to 20 Gb per workstation, which give about an hour's worth of time of edited footage, depending on the resolution and how many digital effects are used.

Media 100 is produced by Media 100 Inc.
www.media100.com

The Complete Animator

The Complete Animator is an 'edutainment' package: a fun animation program for children with cartoon clipart and sounds, a simple toy-like toolkit, and virtual video controls to operate the animation. It works best, we find, if pupils do the drawings for the animation in a separate drawing package – we use the Acorn vector drawing package, *!Draw* – and then import these into the animation software. There they are stamped, with a click of the mouse, in different positions on each frame to make the animation. Backgrounds can be drawn or scanned and imported to run through the whole movie.

What we use it for

Many contexts have a place for this program: ICT lessons, English (a *Macbeth* animation made by Y10 pupils can be seen on the Open University's *Moving Words* website), Maths, Science. The biggest project we use it for is with four partner primary schools. The schools choose a common story to animate (it's *Red Riding Hood* this year), draw backgrounds and storyboards in their schools, then come with their teachers to Parkside to make the animations. The use of the software promotes a wide range of skills – collaborative story and picture-making; media-related design and sequencing skills, and an ability to make multimedia texts which combine image and sound.

Learning outcomes

Specific 'cineliteracy' skills are important, and we teach them explicitly – how to choose between a long or wide shot to establish the forest or the Grandmother's cottage; close-ups on Red Riding Hood's face, or the wolf's head in Granny's nightcap. Also the pace of the narrative, and how animation can control this.

There are also many pleasures experienced by pupils – the pleasure of messing about with a familiar text in animated form; of creating the moving image, still quite a rare experience; and of collaborative work. It's also a pleasure for teachers to watch, for example, a small group of boys, excitedly discovering how they could share their images on a common network space, one boy downloading another's picture and editing part of it into his own. This kind of positive and structured collaboration by boys is, needless to say, very welcome.

Advantages – and a disadvantage

This package is very cheap – about £100 for one program, a bit more for multiple licences (from Iota software in Cambridge). It's very easy to learn, and use, even for quite young children. It's presented as a fun package, very effectively – it's probably the most used piece of software for leisure purposes on our school network, where it attracts large numbers of boys at lunchtimes. Though it's limited, we can also use it in conjunction with other software – it exports films as AVI files, which we have converted to *QuickTime* to edit in *Media 100*. There's also a handy piece of software on the Iota site which will convert bits of animation into animated GIFs for websites. Above all, as I've said, the pupils find it hugely motivating. The only real drawback is that, as computer animation goes, it's very simple, and only really offers two layers – foreground and background. At this level, though, that's all we need.

Complete Animator is made by Iota Software. www.iota.co.uk

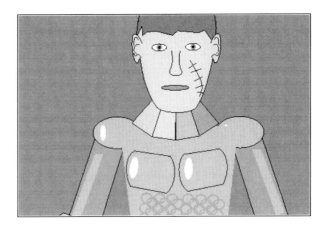

Image of Macbeth from *Complete Animator* film by Year 10 group

Other production software

Backtracks by *bfi*/Illuminations for C4
David Parker, *bfi*

This interactive software package aims to explore how visual media work by offering opportunities to edit pre-selected video images alongside a variety of soundtracks and effects. While the interface is extremely user friendly it still offers ample scope for pupils to fully examine the complexity of visual media and to consider why certain juxtapositions of sound and image are powerfully affective. By dragging and dropping sounds and pictures from the palette window into the edit window it is possible to consider how makers of visual media can build our understanding of what is happening and how audiences actively participate in this process.

Backtracks screen

There are a number of user options within this package. Select 'Freeplay' and gain access to the full library of clips and soundtracks. Or opt instead for one of the 24 graded activities, where your range of archive material will be narrower and which aim to focus on particular styles of media creativity asking learners, for example, to 'Make a Trailer' or 'Build the Mood'.

Backtracks is not only an excellent resource with which to investigate vital elements of film and television – the media which, arguably, still provide us with most of our entertainment and information – it is also a resource Key Stage 3 and 4 teachers would certainly want to use in order to fully exploit our broadening notions of what it means to be fully literate in the information age.

Backtracks includes teaching notes and a detailed reference section. It runs on Windows 95 (but not later Windows versions) and Mac OS 7.5 systems.

Backtracks is available from *bfi* Education (see page 59)

Kidpix Studio by Broderbund
David Parker, *bfi*

This versatile multimedia software uses a number of different tools to allow Key Stage 1 and 2 children to animate, draw, and create sounds and effects either as separate tasks or in any number of combinations. Pupils can make moving image stories using pre-set stamps or by creating original characters and settings using the draw facility.

Pupils' work can be showcased in a 'Slide Show' facility which allows a range of transitional effects to be incorporated – fades, dissolves, split screens etc. Teachers might like to use this software as a way of creating short animated sequences to define or concretise concepts across the curriculum – for example, shape and space in maths. There are a number of pre-set activities designed to reinforce concepts and knowledge across the curriculum which include 'Maths for Fun', 'Make a History Book' and settings using the draw facility.

Alternatively, *Kidpix* could be used to explore questions around moving image media and narrative. A recent bfi research project used this software as a vehicle for the adaptation of Roald Dahl's *Fantastic Mr Fox* by a class of Year 3 pupils. Not only did this class gain a valuable insight into the production of an animated short film, they also found extensive overlap with the teaching and learning outlined in the National Literacy Strategy. Using *Kidpix* certainly made some aspects of language and literacy teaching more accessible to pupils across a wide ability range. *Kidpix* runs on Windows 3.1 or Windows 95 platforms and comes with a straightforward user reference guide, and is widely available.

Picture Power by the English and Media Centre
Rob James, Primary head teacher

Picture Power II is a challenging and powerful sound-and-image editing program on CD-ROM which enables students to create on-screen storyboards complete with voice and music sound tracks.

The stimulus for the storyboards comes from a series of five image banks, from which students can choose sequences of full colour pictures to build a narrative structure. The themed images include *The Bill*, *Mainline Station*, *Pursued*, *Christmas Shopping* and *The Family*. Using a familiar point, drag and drop technique, students can change the order of pictures, crop them to size and alter their duration on-screen. Once the student is satisfied with the storyline, using the same technique, music and sound effects can be added to create and alter atmosphere. To complete the story, a range of transition effects can be added, together with captions and credits. The whole storyboard can then be played back as a slide show. As a bonus, completed work can be printed out for record purposes or off-screen discussion.

It took me less than ten minutes to read the instructions on the cover of the CD-ROM and then master the range of editing techniques. An equally short demonstration enabled my group of Year 6 pupils to be quickly engaged in producing their own storyboard. However, this belies the sophistication of the program, because after mastering the pre-installed sequences, the students can install their own images, music and voice-overs. Up to 64 images can be imported from a scanner, digital camera or clip-art disk and manipulated to create an original sequence.

So *Picture Power* can be used to develop the literacy skills of narrative sequencing of both image and text and the way music and sound affect mood and atmosphere. It would be particularly motivational for less able students. More able students will understand that the same images, music and text can create entirely different messages and feeling depending on how they are edited. This can lead to discussions about bias and tone.

Picture Power II is available from NATE, 50 Broadfield Road, Sheffield S8 OXJ and costs £29.95 or £59.95 for a 5-copy network version, plus £4 post and packing. It will run on a Power Mac with OS 7.5 or later, or a Pentium 90Mhz PC with Windows 95.

iMovie from Apple

Tom Barrance, Media Education, Wales

iMovie video editing software is pre-installed on Apple iMac DV computers. It uses the high-quality 'DV' digital video format. *iMovie* is exceptionally easy to use: you just plug in a compatible DV, miniDV or Digital 8 camcorder and click on an icon to launch the program.

Buttons on the screen control the camcorder. When you've found the clips you want, pressing the 'Import' button makes them appear as small pictures in a grid or 'bin'. Clicking on an image lets you view the clip in a larger window, where you can move through the clip and trim it to length or split it up into sections. You then drag clips into the sequence bar at the bottom of the screen. Here, you can re-arrange them and add sound effects, voice-overs, transitions (like fades and dissolves), music (from CD audio files) and titles or captions. Your film can be exported back to tape or saved in *Quicktime* format for Web or multimedia.

iMovie's interface has been kept very simple, which is the source of most of its limitations. You can't easily insert the image from one clip over the soundtrack of another or edit to the beat of music; editing soundtracks is fiddly; and the on-screen controls for scrubbing through clips and trimming them are too small and easily missed. But these drawbacks are minor when you consider that *iMovie* is the first program that really allows students in an ordinary classroom to follow a complete film-making process, with revisions and amendments being as easy as they are with word-processing or DTP.

Here are some examples:

▶ Over two and a half days, children in a South Wales primary school made a short documentary about their local authority's decision to sell the caretaker's house. They incorporated close-up and wide shots of the house; presentations to camera; interviews with staff and pupils; music; voice-overs, titles and closing credits.
▶ In the space of a morning, a group of primary pupils filmed a class making a frieze. They combined wide shots of the frieze with close-ups of the activities and interviews with children. (The same approach could be used for processes in other subjects, such as a Science experiment or the making and testing of products in Design and Technology.)
▶ In an hour, a lower-ability primary group filmed themselves acting out a confrontation between a boy and a group of bullies (from a book they were reading) and edited it into a 15-second film.

iMovie has a huge number of potential applications across the Primary and Secondary curricula, from video diaries to title sequences, news bulletins, advertisements, travelogues, documentaries, adaptations and information films. We used *iMovie* in its first incarnation, but recently Apple announced

iMovie 2, which allows you to split soundtracks, insert one clip over another the soundtrack of another, and lock it to ensure perfect synchronisation. These modifications should make the new version even more useful in the classroom.

One crucial issue however is the camcorder you use with it. Currently, cheaper camcorders (under £1000) have their 'DV in' facility disabled to avoid EC import duties. This is the facility that *iMovie* uses to control the camera and export sequences to tape. But some cameras can be cheaply adapted to re-activate this facility, and you need to make sure that you can do this with the camcorder you intend to use with *iMovie*. Forthcoming analogue-to-digital converters may allow you to import footage from a non-digital camcorder.

CHAPTER 5

Managing teaching and learning about the moving image

Strategies for planning, recording and implementing moving image work can be grouped into four areas:

▶ **In the classroom** – strategies for supporting pupils' learning with and about moving images.
▶ **In the department** – organising, sharing and evaluating resources.
▶ **In the staffroom** – developing whole school approaches to moving image education.
▶ **In the wider school community** – going public and involving parents, local resources.

These areas will not all be equally significant for you. Some teachers are developing work with moving image more or less on their own. Sometimes this work is pioneered by one department with little interest from the rest of the school. But in some schools – we hope in increasing numbers – it is possible to address this work across the whole school and in its community context as well.

Above:
Holding on to power in 16th century England in *Elizabeth* (Shekhar Kapur, 1997).

Photo: Alex Bailey, courtesy: Polygram

In the classroom

Viewing film or video needs careful planning and preparation if you are to integrate it successfully with the rest of your teaching and get the most out of it. Your task will be much easier if the department or school can make enough basic investment to ensure that screens in classrooms are positioned so that they do not reflect light from windows or overhead lights, that blackout is installed if necessary, that VCRs have efficient pause and frame advance facilities, and that you are provided with a good remote control so that you can operate the pause, fast forward, rewind or play functions from the back of the room. In your planning you can then concentrate on the following six-point checklist.

▶ **Room layout**: Ensure seating arrangements that allow for a clear view of the screen **and** for group work or discussion. Also ensure access to tables or clipboards for notetaking.
▶ **Learning to view**: Watching for pleasure and 'reading' the screen for information, discussion and analysis are different kinds of activity. Pupils need to understand this, and you need to establish ground rules to cover, for example, whether talking during the screening is going to be tolerated, how much notetaking is expected, and exactly what the purpose of the screening is, including any follow-up work you are going to ask for. You must also establish that analysis and discussion must involve interrupted viewing: pauses and repetitions to enable the class to analyse and discuss what they are watching. Pupils will resist this unless its purpose is absolutely clear.

▶ **Defined and explicit aims**: You may be using moving images as a stimulus for ideas, debate, or emotional response; you may wish to exemplify a topic or concept or demonstrate a process. Or your purpose may be to provide a source of evidence, information, data or opinion. In all these cases, moving images are a rich resource which offer many different lines of enquiry and can present ambivalent or contradictory meanings. The more precisely you are able to identify and limit the purpose and intended outcomes of the screening, the more likely it is that pupils will learn from it. It is often wise to focus on two or three substantial learning objectives, rather than trying to draw out a vast range of issues, and it is worth making these explicit to pupils.
▶ **Small group work**: Moving image texts generate productive and lively talk, so it is important to provide time for sharing responses and discussing different perspectives. You could prepare small groups to focus on specific details in the text, which they can discuss after the screening and then share with the rest of the class to build up a broader picture. For example, one group could focus specifically on camerawork, another on sound, another on dialogue or voice-over. Alternatively each group could be given a different statement about the text, or an argument embedded in it, or a single strand or perspective to track and analyse. With some texts it may just be easier to divide up the text chronologically and ask each group to summarise and report back on one section. As always, the structure and composition of small groups need careful review to ensure access and inclusion for all pupils.

▶ **Scaffolding and viewing support**: If your primary aim is to use the moving image as a motivating way of accessing factual data, or to deliver a subject-specific body of knowledge or content, you will probably want to offer some form of information retrieval checklist or prompt to focus attention. However, a comprehension-type worksheet with detailed instructions may be unproductive; close viewing and copious notetaking require competing study skills which are often incompatible, and may be threatening to less confident pupils. In addition, simply using film or video as 'transparent' information media discourages pupils from questioning their techniques, purpose and values – and it is this kind of questioning that lies at the heart of good critical moving image education. You could therefore consider the following techniques in your planning:

  ▷ break the screening down into short sections, each prefaced with a key learning question, which can be discussed in small groups;

  ▷ provide pupils with transcribed extracts, shot lists, sound bites or still images to which they can refer after the screening;

  ▷ prepare pupils with key words, definitions and selected moments to look out for;

  ▷ prepare structured post-screening sheets prompting recall of key issues or data, using cloze procedures, flow diagrams or spidergrams, or sequencing activities.

▶ **Balance of activities**: As with printed texts, pupils need a varied and balanced diet of moving image-related activities. Over-reliance on a few favoured techniques such as freezeframing or storyboarding can become tedious and unproductive. Use the basic teaching techniques grid in Chapter 1 to provide a checklist of possible approaches, and to consider how, when and why you would use them.

In the department

The following checklist of suggestions, drawn from the experiences of departments successfully using moving images, could help you maximise resources and ensure equal access to equipment and materials:

▶ Share and access moving image teaching materials and worksheets in a centrally located area.

▶ Catalogue and store videos, CD Roms and DVDs centrally, with a clear loan system to ensure equal access.

▶ Construct and maintain a departmental advance booking system for hardware including VCRs and monitors, computer technology and video production equipment.

▶ Devise and develop curriculum materials around relevant moving image texts; review existing schemes of work to extend the use of moving images.

▶ Exhibit moving image work produced by students and display their related work such as scripts, storyboards, analyses etc.

▶ Liaise with other departments around collaborative projects or themed work using moving images.

▶ Regular departmental meetings – perhaps termly – set aside to review and evaluate recently acquired moving image material, skills and approaches so that all staff have opportunities to develop their own expertise and identify professional development needs. These meetings in themselves should be seen as an essential aspect of professional development.

Ideally, each department would have a designated responsibility post for the development of moving image education; a more realistic option is probably to share these seven tasks between departmental staff members, with clearly defined areas of responsibility.

A **departmental policy** for moving image will be a luxury for most hard-pressed departments but it may be possible to develop basic departmental guidelines about the range and use of subject-related moving image texts, to ensure comparable practice and agreed policy. This can be useful in terms of issues such as the use of fictional material, the classification of texts according to age-group, function or suitability, and appropriate follow-up activities. It is also sensible to institute a personal loan policy, to allow for catching up on missed screenings or to extend the experience of able or enthusiastic pupils. Most significantly, it is a way of establishing principles about why, when, where and how the department as a whole should contribute to the development of pupils' wider literacy skills. This is of course a whole-school issue, in which your department could lead the way.

Whether or not the moving image aspects of your schemes of work are formally required by your programmes of study, they should be seen as worthy of assessing in their own right if they are to be valued by both students and staff. Record-keeping need not be overly prescriptive or time-consuming, and could take some of the following forms:

▶ A checklist of the types of moving image work to be undertaken by each year group, to ensure progression and continuity.

▶ Incorporating opportunities for moving image work into grids or pro-formas used in outline schemes of work.

▶ Re-designing cover sheets for pupils' work which include reference to the moving image work undertaken, its aims and outcomes, and pupil self-evaluation.

▶ Planning moving image assessment points, when pupils can evaluate their own learning through oral presentation, follow-on writing tasks, or visual presentations.

In the staffroom

Given that the moving image will be used across the school for a variety of learning purposes and outcomes, it seems particularly important for departments to share ideas, resources and policies. Where schools are able to work together towards a **whole school policy**, it can be fruitful to consider a cross-curricular initiative similar to the co-ordination of literacy, perhaps even as part of the literacy co-ordinator's role. The co-ordinator's brief would be to review departmental curricula and policies, and to take overall responsibility for a unified and integrated approach to moving image use both in and out of the classroom. This could cover extra-curricular activities and issues of interest to parents and to the wider community. Where this is not feasible, the following shorter-term strategies can be considered:

▶ **Departmental alliances**: departments with shared moving image interests could link creative production work in Art, English and ICT; using moving image as evidence in History and English; animation work drawing on Maths, Music and Science; using role-play and video in Performing Arts and Humanities, and so on. These sorts of alliances are often best initiated on a small scale in the staffroom, piloted informally, and then incorporated into subject curricula more formally once tried and tested.

▶ **In-service Training**: set aside a training day session for whole-school INSET or departmental workshops on topics such as the use of moving image software, practical skills in moving image analysis, developing a cross-curricular project or for general forward planning.

▶ **A moving image education group or workshop**: a voluntary group consisting of representatives from different departments to meet on a half-termly or monthly basis for discussion of moving image issues, the sharing of practice, the screening of interesting or contentious moving image texts etc.

▶ **Enrichment initiatives for pupils**: out of school hours funding can be used to offer pupils more extended and intensive opportunities for watching or making moving image texts, through video or film clubs, video production groups, and cinema visits. See also Chapter 7 for resources and screening providers.

British Transport films of the 1950s promoted the power and beauty of the railways. *This is York* (J.B.Holmes, 1953) in the video compilation *This Sceptred Isle – Yorkshire* (British Transport Films 1952-62) available from *bfi* Video.

Courtesy: bfi Stills

In the wider community

Film and television are unique as teaching and learning resources in that their potential impact is as powerful outside the school as inside it: often they are more highly valued in the wider community than in the curriculum. But popular misconceptions about moving image education have been fuelled by previous governments and by the press, so that parents, governors and local media may be prejudiced against it. This can be countered by:

▶ Displaying and/or screening pupils' work at Parents' and Open Evenings.

▶ Arranging public screenings, for example at a local cinema, of pupils' production work, to which local primary schools, parents, governors and local media are invited.

▶ Open evenings for parents on the use of different teaching and learning styles within the school, focusing on the use of moving image media.

▶ Guidelines for parents about the different ways in which their children may be using the moving image in class and for homework, and accessible school-to-home materials so that they can understand and effectively support their children's home viewing.

▶ Exploring the resources and moving image expertise that parents and relatives can bring to the school.

▶ Making contact with local cinemas, media organisations, libraries, further education colleges, film and video workshops, to negotiate relevant visits, screenings, work experience placements and curriculum support (see Chapter 7).

CHAPTER 6

Becoming Cineliterate – learning progression
Towards a model of learning progression

Because little consistent and continuing moving image education currently takes place in schools, there is a lack of shared and explicit sense of the standard of work that might be expected at different stages. Anecdotal evidence suggests that similar kinds of moving image activity may be required of pupils at widely differing age levels, with similar results. Teachers' ideas about appropriate levels of challenge in either critical or creative moving image work tend to be derived from their experience elsewhere in the curriculum rather than from continuing experience of moving image activities with pupils of different ages. This is not surprising, given the general lack of in-service training and advisory support for any kind of media education.

There is therefore a clear need for a model to stimulate thinking about how pupils' learning might be expected to progress over several years if their moving image education were sustained consistently. Any such model needs to be firmly based in classroom practice and teachers' own research if it is to have any credibility. But a start has to be made somewhere, which is why we provide here a hypothetical model which some teachers, departments and schools may wish to use as a framework for discussion and reflection.

This model was first published in *Making Movies Matter*, the report of the Film Education Working Group (*bfi* 1999). It attempts to show what might be the outcomes of learning about the moving image media of film, video and television (FVT) through five stages of learning progression. These stages can be mapped on to the stages of mandatory and post-16 education, but the model can also be seen as non-age-specific, and all learners would to some extent pass through these stages. It is also a cumulative model: learners in Stage 5 would still be using the same keywords and doing the same kinds of activity that were identified at Stage 1, but in a context of more sophisticated usage and wider viewing experience.

No course content is shown here: this is not a syllabus or a curriculum. For the sake of conciseness and simplicity the model uses quite general terms and is very basic. It is divided into two broad sections at each level: **Experiences and Activities**, which provides an indication of the range of inputs learners would need, and **Outcomes**, which describes what learners should be able to do by the end of the stage. At each stage a list of **Key Words** is provided, **not** as a vocabulary to be taught, but as a way of suggesting the areas and types of knowledge that each stage might involve.

The model is based upon three broad conceptual areas, for which a more detailed rationale can be found on page 57:

▶ **The language of moving images** – focusing on the ways in which moving image texts are internally *constructed*;
▶ **Producers and audiences** – exploring the ways in which moving image texts are *made and delivered* to audiences;
▶ **Messages and values** – concerned with the *interpretations* of the world offered by moving image texts and the effects these may have.

To become a really useful guide to teaching and learning, this model needs critical engagement from practising teachers. This can only happen where individuals and departments are able to invest in the necessary time for reflection and analysis, which of course will depend upon very particular circumstances. The *bfi* will seek to foster these over the next few years and to encourage others to do the same. Education departments in higher education and in other agencies may wish to use it as the basis for research, curriculum development and teacher training. Some schools – perhaps specialist schools in particular – may be able to undertake valuable developmental work on this model within the classroom, and to share it with others. The *bfi* is keen to hear about such work and to help disseminate it.

**Above:
Imagined worlds: the final sequence
of Lynne Ramsay's *Ratcatcher* (1999).**
Courtesy: Pathe

Becoming Cineliterate · Stage 1

Pupils should have opportunities to:

▶ See a wide range of film, video and television (FVT) from different world cultures including different styles of animation, live action drama, adventure, musical, abstract, factual, documentary; short films and features; historical and contemporary, home videos.
▶ Access moving images in different ways, eg cinema, video, television, video games, CD-ROM.
▶ Talk about out-of-school FVT viewing, responses and preferences.
▶ Talk about content and structure of short video sequences while teacher uses pause button to encourage and enable close observation of compostion and framing.
▶ Use VCR, camcorder, and ICT software for sequencing and making animations.

Key Words

shot	longshot	film
cut	pan	television
fade	track	videotape
mix	focus	programme
zoom	soundtrack	animation
close-up	special effects	video recorder
mid-shot	cinema	camcorder

Learners should be able to:

Language

▶ Identify and talk about structuring features such as music, changes in location, interior/exterior settings, actors and presenters.
▶ Use Key Words to refer to elements of film language when describing events in a story.
▶ Use Key Words in talking about character types, as well as referring to clues such as dress, casting, performance etc.

Producers and Audiences

▶ Use credits, video covers and posters to identify titles and actors' names, likely audience category, and theme or genre.
▶ Identify broad categories of intended audience, eg 'this is for little children', and give reasons.
▶ Identify common features between FVT, book and game versions of generic texts, eg myth, fairy tale, space adventure etc.

Messages and Values

▶ Identify and talk about different levels of 'realism', eg naturalistic drama vs cartoon animation.
▶ Use Key Words to refer to elements of film language when explaining personal responses and preferences.
▶ Identify devices such as flashback, dream sequences, exaggeration – discuss why they are needed and how they are conveyed.

In addition they should be able to:

▶ Use VCR to find and repeat short sequences of FVT to support analysis and discussion.
▶ Work co-operatively with others to discuss or make moving image sequences.
▶ Use ICT software to sequence still or moving images to tell story or convey information.
▶ Transfer a narrative sequence from one medium to another, eg poem to film/photo story; film sequences to written text or cartoon strip.
▶ Add music or commentary to a moving image sequence.

Becoming Cineliterate · Stage 2

EXPERIENCES AND ACTIVITIES

Pupils should have opportunities to:

▶ See a wide range of FVT including more narratively complex stories, more from pre-1950 and silent periods, films from different cultures including subtitled films, and non-narrative and experimental films.
▶ Watch and discuss sequences that build impressions or emotional effects, eg montage.
▶ See different versions of the same story or event.
▶ Watch/listen and discuss the use of music, voices, sound effects and silence in short sequences.
▶ Watch and discuss how continuities and discontinuities in space and time are conveyed in FVT (eg in chase sequences).
▶ Watch and discuss sequences in which characters are presented non-verbally (eg through camera position, lighting, costume, music etc).

Key Words

angle	broadcast	recorded
frame	channel	censorship
sequence	release	classification
dialogue	exhibitor	budget
sound effects	trailer	'watershed'
projector	feature	star
scriptwriter	short	satellite
script	documentary	cable
composer	live action	
director	live	

OUTCOMES

Learners should be able to:

Language

▶ Describe how sound contributes to the overall meaning of a moving image sequence, using Key Words where appropriate.
▶ Use Key Words to explain how a FVT sequence is constructed.

Producers and Audiences

▶ Use Key Words to distinguish between different moving image delivery systems.
▶ Identify and distinguish some production roles, using Key Words.
▶ Suggest reasons why different people may have different responses to the same FVT text.
▶ Explain why some FVT may cost a lot of money to make.

Messages and Values

▶ Use Key Words to identify ways in which FVT can show things that have not 'really' happened, eg violence, magic.
▶ Explore reasons for and against censorship, age classification and the broadcasting 'watershed'.

In addition they should be able to:

▶ Read subtitles.
▶ Plan and shoot short sequences on video using more than one point of view, eg a person entering a room; one person meeting another; a chase.
▶ Create animated sequences on film, video or ICT or in an optical toy such as a zoetrope.

Becoming Cineliterate · Stage 3

Pupils should have opportunities to:

▶ See a wide range of FVT including examples of different national cinemas of different historical periods, examples of major directors and significant 'movements'.
▶ Watch and discuss sequences which have ambiguous elements or do not have a clear narrative resolution.
▶ Through analysis and practical activity, explore ways in which small editorial changes can effect meaning (eg slight change of timing of a cut).
▶ Look at and discuss publicity material for films and have opportunities to make posters, press packs, trailers etc.
▶ Use interviews and questionnaires to find out about audiences choices and preferences.

Key Words

editor	copyright	unrealistic
cinematographer	scheduling	non-realistic
distributor	narrowcast	non-narrative
production	genre	abstract
company	realism	stereotype
target market	realistic	marketing
profit	authentic	promotion
ratings	propaganda	
box office	representation	

Learners should be able to:

Language

▶ Use Key Words to identify and discuss differences between FVT genres.
▶ Explain how meaning is created through editing of image and sound.
▶ Explain some of the ways in which film styles have changed over time.

Producers and Audiences

▶ Identify and distinguish between a wider range of production roles.
▶ Explain basic differences between processes of pre-production, production, post-production and exhibition.
▶ Use Key Words to explain some of the ways FVT are marketed and promoted to audiences.
▶ Identify and discuss factors that may contribute to success of a FVT text, eg star, genre, theme.

Messages and Values

▶ Use Key Words to explain how social groups, events and ideas are represented in FVT.
▶ Explain and justify aesthetic judgements and personal responses.
▶ Argue for alternative ways of representing a group, event or idea.

In addition they should be able to:

▶ Use ICT to draft, create and manipulate moving image and sound sequences.
▶ Use online and print resources to access information about films.
▶ Use credits, packaging and publicity material to identify key information about a film's production.

Becoming Cineliterate · Stage 4

Pupils should have opportunities to:

▶ See a range of FVT that both consolidates and extends existing viewing experience in terms of genre, directors, national cinemas, mainstream and non-mainstream, historical periods.
▶ Find out more about different modes of FVT production, eg industrial/mainstream vs low-budget independent.
▶ Have opportunities to relate FVT knowledge to other cultural fields, eg literature, history, fine art, music etc.
▶ Investigate a topic, using FVT text, online and print sources.

Key Words

deep focus	dominant	theme
montage	independent	style
hand-held camera	low budget	16mm
auteur	avant-garde	35mm
art cinema	surrealist	digital
Hollywood	expressionist	non-linear
ideology	*cinéma vérité*	analogue
mainstream	*mise en scène*	

Learners should be able to:

Language

▶ Identify and describe some major FVT styles and narrative forms, using Key Words.
▶ Explain how elements of FVT styles may relate to technologies, eg portable cameras, editing software.

Producers and Audiences

▶ Identify and discuss some of the factors in the production process that may effect the final shape and meaning of a FVT text.
▶ Describe some of the risks and costs involved in FVT production, distribution and exhibition.
▶ Explain some of the possibilities and limitations of audience research.

Messages and Values

▶ Use Key Words to discuss and evaluate FVT texts with strong social or ideological messages.

In addition they should be able to:

▶ Use ICT to redraft and manipulate moving image and sound sequences in response to audience comment.
▶ Use FVT knowledge to evaluate information on FVT from online and print sources.
▶ Use stills and clips in live or recorded presentations of critical arguments or investigations.

Becoming Cineliterate · Stage 5

EXPERIENCES AND ACTIVITIES

Pupils should have opportunities to:

▶ Use ICT to explore expressive/communicative potential of specific FVT styles.
▶ Consolidate viewing experience and background knowledge of two or three aspects of FVT, eg a genre, a director's work, or a movement, a national cinema, a technological innovation.
▶ Read and discuss some critical approaches to FVT, eg auteur, genre, realism, audience effects, representation etc.
▶ Undertake independent research, using FVT texts, online and print sources, and live interviews where appropriate.

Key Words

theory	hegemony	diegesis
critical	intertextuality	institution
culture	aesthetic	

OUTCOMES

Learners should be able to:

Language

▶ Explain how FVT styles and narrative forms can relate to authors, production context, social and cultural context.
▶ Use film language to construct moving image narratives.
▶ Identify and describe the contributions of different skills in a FVT text.

Producers and Audiences

▶ Describe and explain how authors, genres and stars are meaning-bearing systems and how they can be used to market FVT.
▶ Identify and describe some of the ways in which FVT institutions relate to social, cultural and political contexts.
▶ Describe the economic organisation of FVT institutions and the relationship between producers, distributors, exhibitors and audiences.

Messages and Values

▶ Use Key Words to discuss and evaluate ideological messages in mainstream FVT texts.
▶ Describe and account for different levels of realism in FVT texts.
▶ Explain relationships between aesthetic style and social/political meaning.

In addition they should be able to:

▶ Assemble research findings into clear argument or exposition.
▶ Create moving image texts for specific audiences and purposes in specific styles and genres.
▶ Develop independent judgements about the value and relevance of critical theories.

Further Learning

In specialist higher and continuing education, learners will develop increased ability to research independently, to synthesise ideas and information across a range of areas and to speculate and argue on the basis of such syntheses, to develop their understanding of FVT study as a discipline and to write, speak and make FVT within the disciplinary paradigm.

Rationale

Language

Each medium has its own system of conveying meaning, although schools have concentrated mainly on the medium of print. But over the last 100 years, the moving image medium of film has developed a particularly powerful language, which is now also used by television, video and computer software. The ways in which images are framed, sequenced, paced and combined with sounds – music and sound effects as well as words – have become a highly significant component of the information, stories and ideas we encounter every day. Everyone should have the chance to learn about how the moving image media create meaning. It is a basic skill of cineliteracy to be able to refer to devices such as framing, camera angle or editing easily and meaningfully in discussion and in critical writing. People of any age learn this most easily when they have opportunities to make and manipulate these devices in their own creative work.

Courtesy: *bfi* Stills

Fifty years before Disney, Jean Marais brought the Beast to life in *La Belle et la Bête* (Jean Cocteau 1946).

Producers and Audiences

Now that there are so many different sources of communication it is an increasingly important element of basic citizenship for people to be able to identify where messages are coming from and what motivates them. It is not enough simply to be able to interpret or create moving image texts. The moving image media are huge industries and films are commodities, bought and sold by competing multinational companies. Audiences are targeted and courted in many different ways, although their real interests and responses can be very hard to identify. Everyone should be able to make informed choices about their consumption of moving image media, learning how to identify their sources and the interests they serve. By recognising that they themselves are members of audiences and larger social groups, learners can think about how their own interests relate to the ways they are defined by others. They should experience the excitement and power of producing their own moving image texts and these should be seen and discussed by real audiences.

Perceptions of the British Empire are renegotiated in Richard Attenborough's *Gandhi* (1982).

Messages and Values

Film and television can affect our emotions and our ideas. There are many theories about the effects of the moving image and opinion is fundamentally divided as to the real extent of its power to affect behaviour. However, we all know that we can be moved, entranced, angered, delighted or bored by film and it is important to explore these responses and be able to justify them. Particular texts or types of text may have ongoing effects on our ideas, values and beliefs: we need to consider whether this is the case, how it happens and whether it matters. It is also important to think about how we might assess the potential effects of the moving image – whether these are aesthetic, moral, political or economic – on other individuals and groups. Everyone should be able to explore the relative realism of different moving image texts and have learned to distinguish between literal meanings and underlying themes. Learners should have the chance both to see and to create moving image texts in a variety of modes from documentary and dramatic realism to fantasy and non-narrative forms.

Courtesy: *bfi* Stills